SECRET SOCIETY

Emma Nicholson

SECRET SOCIETY

INSIDE – AND OUTSIDE – THE CONSERVATIVE PARTY

INDIGO

First published in Great Britain 1996
as an Indigo paperback original

Indigo is an imprint of the Cassell Group
Wellington House, 125 Strand, London WC2R 0BB

A catalogue record for this book is
available from the British Library.

ISBN 0 575 40072 2

Designed and typeset by
Production Line, Minster Lovell, Oxford
Printed and bound in Great Britain by
Cox & Wyman Ltd, Reading, Berks

96 97 98 99   10 9 8 7 6 5 4 3 2 1

Contents

Acknowledgements

I am grateful to my constituency secretary Ruth Manning, with whom I have worked in close partnership for eight years, for all the hard work she has put in to help me produce this book.

Too many other people have given assistance, through thoughts, research or letters, for me to name them here. I am grateful to them all and I have no doubt that, singly or together, we will continue to debate the important political issues of our times.

It has been a satisfying challenge to work with three specialist professionals, namely Derek Johns, a director of literary agency A. P. Watt, Sean Magee, senior commissioning editor at Victor Gollancz, and Gillian Bromley, a freelance editor. I have learned much from them.

My thanks are offered also to those people who wrote to me after I had taken my decision to join the Liberal Democrat Party. Some of their thoughts are reproduced in the Epilogue.

Introduction

No science ever attains perfection. No system ever arrives
at finality. The progress of civilisation, the development
of human intellect, the increase of knowledge and
experience, the growth of national life – all tend to
render obsolete those sciences and established systems
which yesterday may have been thought to be perfect. It
is necessarily and naturally so. Changed conditions
demand new methods, revision of existing ones.
Necessity stimulates invention . . . Principles, on the other
hand, if sound, remain unchanged.

> Preface to *Principles and Practice of the System of Control over*
> *Parliamentary Grants* by Colonel A. J. V. Durrell CB (1917)

This elegant exposition of the relation of means to ends in
parliamentary affairs pinpoints what is wrong with the
Conservative Party of the 1990s. No longer are the mechanisms
of government operated in the pursuit of sound principles and
core values; they have now been turned to the service of their
own perpetuation. Principles have been subsumed by methods;
values consumed by iconoclastic practice.

Perhaps the last word on the state of the Tory Party today is
best expressed in a comment on change to be found in the
preface to the 1549 *Book of Common Prayer* of the Church of
England, an institution which the Conservatives for so long
mistakenly believed they owned – and one which, when the
reality of the Church's views on the Government's social
policies emerged in the mid-1980s, they then chose to attack.

The passage runs: 'There was never anything . . . so well devised, or so sure established, which in . . . time hath not been corrupted.'

In absolute terms of the standards required by successive electorates of Members of the Mother of Parliaments, the present Conservative Party has collectively fallen from grace by choice. It is difficult to avoid the word 'corrupted' in an accurate description of the behaviour of a fair number of MPs with regard to the scale of their outside earnings and to the political work triggered by their paymasters. It is also the appropriate term to use of the Government, with its disregard of the boundary formerly observed between the party from which it comes and the actions of the state on behalf of the nation.

Corruption is socially corrosive and destructive of healthy, benign organizations. It should be fought strenuously wherever it is found, both as a matter of principle and in practice. Personal or cultural greed may be the largest element in the corruption of any political body. It is certainly seen as the least desirable political attribute by electors, for this is the motive which puts their needs last, not first, in line for the attention, resources and wisdom they seek from those they elect to represent them.

'Fight from within' – and silently, as far as the outside world is concerned: this is the whispered slogan of the secrecy-obsessed modern Conservative Party. In consequence, in its corrupted state, the party in government has become a secret society, funded by the public purse, working now only to keep itself in power.

Chapter 1

Breaking Point

Physical assault by a member of one's own party is not an everyday hazard of voting in the House of Commons. So I was the more taken aback when, having for the first time voted against the Government in a division, I felt someone push roughly past me as I stood in the crowd near the Serjeant at Arms and hit me, hard, in the stomach. It was an angry Tory member – a 'colleague' of mine – resorting to violence in outrage at my having taken at face value the evening's 'free vote'. The date was 6 November 1995, and I had just passed through the 'Aye' lobby to support an amendment, strenuously opposed by the Government, which would have forced disclosure by MPs of a small part of their extra-parliamentary earnings.

With hindsight, the Nolan vote was my breaking point. The conduct of the vote, its outcome and its immediate aftermath began the unravelling of my emotional, historical and personal ties to the Conservative Party. Once loosened, the threads binding me fell away very rapidly, and seven weeks later, on Gladstone's birthday, I joined the Liberal Democrats. I found that I had come home.

The passage, if brief, was painful: and the physical blow was merely the beginning. I approached the Whips to ask what I should do about the person who had struck me. It had been a deliberate assault, forceful enough to cause me to double up. Members were not allowed to hit each other in the Chamber. I walked up to the pairing Whip in search of counsel. Instead, I was taken to task for voting against the Government. I was stunned. It had been a free vote, I answered; what was the point of a free vote? Had it not been a free vote?

I quickly went back into the voting lobby, now clear of Members. Sitting at the open desk I dipped the pen nib into the inkwell and took a piece of Commons paper from the rack – choosing that marked with the neutral green portcullis, not the party coloured blue or red. I wrote to the Whip from whom I had just parted, asking him to explain: was or was not a free vote a free vote? As an ordinary backbencher I was entitled, within Commons rules (admittedly unwritten), to exercise my vote on free vote issues exactly as I chose. I was not subject to any whip. That was the very meaning of the phrase 'free vote' printed – now rarely – on the weekly whipping lists. If the Whips wished to force people to vote in a particular way, they had the capacity to make a directive. A free vote signified the absence of any such directive. I took my letter into the Whips' Office and left it on his desk. I never received a reply.

As I walked towards Central Lobby, making for my own office at Millbank, another Whip stopped me and told me I had lost the Conservative Party the general election. I asked why.

'Because,' he replied, 'good colleagues will leave, as they will no longer be able to earn as much money as they wish. Other colleagues in marginal seats will lose at the election since the public will discover how they have been earning extra pay.'

I answered that, since the public were paying us all to be their Members of Parliament, if those colleagues were earning additional pay in a way of which the public did not approve, they should leave at once. The Whip's only response to this was to repeat that I had lost the Government the general election. I was bewildered.

Earlier on the day of the vote I had found myself arguing with Lord Dahrendorf, the Warden of St Antony's College, Oxford, about the impending vote on the role and conduct of MPs. I told him plainly that the existing situation was conning companies, leading them to believe that if they paid a Member of Parliament, they would get something they could not get otherwise. This was just not true; moreover, it was essential that it should not be true. No duty can or should be able to be performed by a Member of Parliament for additional pay that cannot or should not be performed by any one of us for nothing. In the end, we agreed. I left the college to catch the train back to London for the vote.

On my way to the Chamber I was stopped in the passage by a former Government minister. 'I hear you may not be going to vote with us tonight,' he boomed. I replied that I was not. I had given evidence to the Nolan Committee, as he knew, and was going to support its recommendations. 'Ah,' he said, 'you should support the Prime Minister. He has told us to vote with the Select Committee's proposals.'

I said, 'I am supporting the Prime Minister. I am doing precisely what he told us to do in July – "embrace the spirit of Nolan", take on the whole report. I am sorry that in the Select Committee you did not apparently listen to him. The Prime Minister got it right then; it's not my mistake that he has got it wrong now. He should not have contradicted himself. He should have stuck by his original perception.'

An argument ensued. My antagonist said furiously: 'I suppose it doesn't matter to you. You are a kept woman.'

I said: 'How could this vote matter to you? You have inherited wealth. You should know better.'

The vote was called; but still I was not to get to the Division Lobby unchallenged. In the crush of Members pushing towards the Chamber between the two standing, black-clad Messengers, my arm was caught urgently by the Party Chairman, Brian Mawhinney. He was moving in the opposite direction, and he was smiling, revealing a chilling array of tombstone teeth. I had seldom seen him smile off camera; nor could I remember his ever approaching me before. 'Come and talk with me,' he said.

I demurred: 'The vote has already been called.'

'But come and have coffee and we can discuss the vote,' he urged.

'We'll miss it if we do,' I said. 'I'll happily have coffee with you afterwards.' He was still pressing me, pulling me against the flow of Members going to vote, and I had to break free physically to join them. No coffee was on offer afterwards.

Just outside the Division Lobby a glowering figure stood alone by a pillar, noting the Conservatives who came through against the Government; the Whips, on the same errand, were anxiously and furiously scanning faces. I, too, was looking around, with rather different motives. Surely the Lobby was not full enough for the 'yes' vote to win. There were Liberal Democrat and Labour Members aplenty; but where were the other Conservatives? Without them, all was lost. As we approached the vote desk, I could not think that we had won. Passing the clerk, I gave my name and he marked it off. A personal watershed had passed: for the first time, I was supporting an Opposition amendment against the known position of the Government. I recalled a comment of my father's: 'Don't do it until you really mean it.' I did.

The results of the vote were not long in coming. I was flooded with relief. Just enough Conservatives had been prepared to venture into the 'Aye' Lobby. There were twenty-one of us: a magnificent number, and yet tiny by comparison with the whole Cabinet and Government and the large majority of Tory backbenchers, all of whom voted against full disclosure of earnings which I would regard as at best open to question and at worst improper.

And yet, even after the passage of a very limited measure, the Tories were in turmoil. It was an astounding scene. Their cloak of superiority had been stripped away to reveal the greed beneath. Among those who opposed the vote on limited dis-closure, some were the already rich who wanted to get richer; greedy above their worth to Parliament, they had no intention of removing their snouts from the trough. Avarice and panic

made an unattractive cocktail as they saw the pound signs
floating past their eyes. What was to become of the company
delegations they took to meet ministers, paid for by the
businesses? What was to become of their lucrative contracts?
Others began quickly to regroup and address themselves to
damage limitation. We will renegotiate our contracts, they were
saying. The amendment passed was only about paid work as a
result of being a Member of Parliament. If we have a contract
for a hundred thousand pounds, we can say that only one
thousand pounds of that is related to being a Member of
Parliament. As I listened, I reached the extraordinary conclusion that I could stay with these people no longer; worse still, I
did not even wish my name to be associated with theirs. The
logic of my conclusion was inescapable: I could not stand again
as a Conservative Member of Parliament.

As I stood there in sorrow, Richard Shepherd, a fellow
Conservative, dashed up to me. He had seen another opportunity, and said to me: 'Now we have to vote to keep down the
salary of the Parliamentary Commissioner for Standards, the
Ombudsman.'

To my mind, this was quite the reverse of what was needed.
'No, Richard,' I said, 'to deal with these people we have to have
someone eminent enough to stand up to them and face them
down, and on a salary appropriate to that task.'

For me, the Nolan Committee had identified tasks whose
importance set them above party squabbles and across party
lines. There was a piece of work to be done: not just for us, but
for the next generation, the parliamentarians of the future. It
was a poor reflection on the prevailing standards that the
Government had had to appoint a committee under a Law
Lord to itemize the conduct to be expected of MPs; but it was
a relief that the nettle appeared to have been grasped. Sadly, I
was to discover that I had overestimated the Government's
willingness to maintain that grasp. At first, in May 1995, the
Prime Minister had announced that he was accepting not just

the Nolan Report in its entirety but, as he put it rather effusively, the 'spirit' of Nolan too. He had then turned turtle and, the following month, announced that a special Standing Committee was to be set up to examine Nolan's recommendations and report back to Parliament. I was dismayed. This, I felt, would be the kiss of death. The committee would be given secret instructions through the Conservative Whips' Office; the Government, of course, would have a built-in majority on the committee – that is the system; and the chairman of the committee would be Tony Newton MP, Leader of the House of Commons and therefore bound to follow the Government line. I had told the Whips immediately that I was likely to vote against the setting up of the committee, for I saw this as a very important issue. We were legislating on the ethics of Members. We had been given a chance to clean up the modern House of Commons, secure the base of high ethical standards created by earlier generations of Members and leave that heritage intact for those who would succeed us. We could seek to mark down 1995 as a year equal to 1832 in the fight against corruption.

By the time the Select Committee on Standards in Public Life had made its second report at the end of October 1995, I had disengaged myself personally from the Government's vast train of dependants in order to be able to fight this issue cleanly. Indeed, I was already exploring career options outside politics. I took great satisfaction in the achievements of three voluntary organizations which I chaired – on access for the disabled, on jobs and training for the young blind, and on refugees – and my domestic happiness was, to my profound astonishment and delight, continuously increasing.

Earlier in the year, on 24 January 1995, I had put my views on record in evidence to Lord Nolan and his Committee. My evidence was simple, and it had been taken into the body of the Committee's proposals. I had said that public respect for Parliament would only be restored if Members of the House of

Commons gave up some of their sources of extra income, particularly earnings from the multi-client lobbying world. I had also said that Members would honour a new code setting standards of personal morality – and in that I had just been proved wrong. The vote of 6 November saw my confidence in the commitment of my Conservative colleagues to honourable dealing dissolve, along with any scraps of faith I still retained, contrary to my own experience, in the ethical standards, or even honest judgement, of the Whips. For twenty years I had been an active Conservative politician – first as a Prospective Parliamentary Candidate, next as Party Vice-Chairman, then as a Member of the House of Commons; but now the party had lost its claim on my loyalty. I'd given it the benefit of the doubt much too often.

I hadn't been overly idealistic in my expectations of the House of Commons when I embarked on a political career in the 1970s. I didn't think then that MPs were all squeaky clean, irreproachable in all their dealings: politics – for my generation, at least – was inevitably a tarnished business. But politics in 1995 – this grubby, personal, cash-grasping degeneration of the body politic, brazen in its cynicism – was something different, and something insupportable. I had in fact been disturbed by the attitude of Members of Parliament towards both expense claims and outside earnings shortly after I joined the House of Commons. I was used to standard business practice, whereby annotated invoices were required to support all claims for money that had been spent. I soon discovered that MPs' mileage claims were not subject to that normal check, unless a monthly ceiling of 500 miles was exceeded. The top mileage rate was 74p in summer 1996. Our free first-class rail or air ticket created no equivalent cash bonus. Hence the car travel boom.

Hitherto I had stuck to the old-established Conservative precept: support the Government in public, and if your own views differ, make them known in private and so influence outcomes behind the scenes. That was the party's way of going about its business, the loyal, accepted method to which I had bound myself on joining it. But this method no longer worked. Its success for the supplicant backbencher – and therefore for the health of party debate – rested on three things: first, an effective team of Whips who knew their charges and deserved respect as well as fear; second, a well-knit and well-informed team of ministers who knew both their departmental tasks and their party's political goals, and were sufficiently able to pursue both while listening and responding to the needs of constituencies and the wider public interest; and third, a Prime Minister of sufficient personal and political stature. Even the *primus inter pares* system beloved of the Tories could not work well – or, indeed, at all – without effective leadership.

None of these three existed in the Conservative Party of 1995. For us backbenchers, the Whips held the key to the system; their failure affected all of us. And they had indeed failed us. The South West Whip – my Whip for the last six months of my time in the Conservative Party – was Gary Streeter from Plymouth; so far from incorporating in his game plan my constituents' needs as perceived by me, their elected representative, he did not once speak to me on anything at all during that time. Perhaps it was not surprising that they should have become so detached from ordinary Members and their concerns, given the rapidity of turnover in the Whips' Office. This was now a ministerial recruiting ground, a pool of candidates for offices of state. All Government appointments are made by the Chief Whip and the Prime Minister: that is why the job of Chief Whip is so attractive. It is the best spot behind the throne. The new Whips were largely young and relatively inexperienced, incapable of inspiring respect. Whips are often compared to school prefects; now they were more like teacher's pet sneak than Head of House. Outside the Commons, I heard senior industrialists and City of London financiers express their astonishment at the quality of these men, and of ministers too.

Something was rotten in the Conservative Party.

Ministers lacked cohesion, even coherence. Although their weekend crib hymn sheets, handed out by the head of the Conservative Research Department in Central Office, strove to identify a selection of chords for them to strike in public state- ments, there was no theme tune on which they could compose their departmental variations. As the Prime Minister shifted his stance – sometimes more than once within twenty-four hours on a single issue – so the ministerial chorus line swayed hestitat- ingly left, right, backwards, forwards, finally shuffling untidily towards a different corner of the stage. Amusing it might be, but it wasn't the kind of politics I could admire.

And the Prime Minister was no leader. Quick on his feet, with a winning spontaneity of style, he had no vision, no plan; he inspired neither personal attachment among his closer colleagues nor confidence among the wider parliamentary party or the public. Nobody trusted him to take the right decision, or to stick to any decision, once taken, on anything. His was the politics of expediency: he held on tight while the roller-coaster bucketed up and down the steep inclines of events and circum- stances, but he wasn't the driver. That seat was vacant and there was no dead man's brake.

Supporting the Government became impossible with the rapid changes of position at the top. I curtailed my public state- ments drastically after one particular episode. The Prime Minister and Michael Heseltine had announced a difficult policy decision on mining one evening. On one particular point I had supported them on the following morning's *Today* programme; I knew that my own position was well founded, having first checked with Labour Members, who implicitly supported the Government's position on this specific point. By eleven o'clock that same morning, frightened by the headlines, the Government had changed its mind.

All this reduced backbench MPs to the status of rubber stamps. Our job, as a Chief Whip once angrily ordered me, was to support the Government's policy: any policy, on anything, whether or not we knew anything about it or had even heard it identified before. But Members are not conscripts, and their political hearts should belong to the people. Our constituents' voices could only be heard in the corridors of power if we were able to speak for them. Certainly, as a general rule, MPs must support their parties; since the Executive is located in the House of Commons, if this were not the norm, the Government could fall every day and the system would collapse. But MPs must also be able to use all of Parliament's great influence to better their constituents' lives.

It seemed to me, too, that constituents were becoming aware that they were being short-changed. I had felt for some time that the public wanted more of the Conservative Government than it was prepared to give – including, at the top of the list, higher standards of work plus a restoration, or at least a re-examination, of political ethics. They didn't want nostalgia. Nor did they just want a change of governing party, though clearly a surface tension existed which sought the release of an election. The dissatisfaction went deeper, building to a demand for more profound change, for a review of our entire political system in general and our electoral system in particular. It seemed to me that the electorate had been pondering the failure of the system to give it adequate governance and coming to the conclusion that a different electoral system might do better, producing MPs whose world was closer to their own. Proportional representation, even the alternative vote, might lance the boil. Demand for electoral reform was far from new; even Winston Churchill had advocated a move to either PR or the alternative vote. But now there was a wider sense outside Westminster that it was not just people but structures that had to change. As Ian Aitken pointed out in an article for the *New Statesman* in January 1996, 'Major and his ministers are almost literally going about the country with an axe, hacking at the fabric of our society as if they wanted to damage it beyond

repair before being forced to hand it over to Labour . . . in
military terminology that's called a scorched earth policy. Is that
what Majorism has come to mean?' It was not just the
Government's overwhelming power that Aitken highlighted, but
its incompetence too: it was, he said, 'almost slapstick, custard
pie, food in the bucket . . . an assembly of seedy clowns.'

In a nutshell, the British were not getting the government
they deserved. This was only too apparent to me inside the
House of Commons Chamber. John Major's 'back to basics'
campaign of 1993 had been designed to reinstate the
Government and the Conservative Party as the guardians of
principle in the public eye. In fact, it was the Conservative
parliamentary party itself that lay at the heart of the sleaze that
oozed through the Commons. John Major's speech writers were
trying to paste a veneer of respectability over a worm-ridden
core. The public were not fooled. To their mind it was the
politicians who needed to get 'back to basics'.

This failure of political ethics to measure up to public expectations was not exclusive to Britain; elsewhere in Europe, too,
similar disillusionment was apparent as too few politicians were
seen to be working for the public good. However, I now saw
that the problem was particularly acute in Britain and, within
Britain, in the Conservative Party. For too many MPs, any
underlying or original desire to serve the public had been
overlaid or displaced by a drive for personal gain. Within
the hothouse atmosphere of the Commons, greed seemed
infectious.

What was the motive for this accelerating rapacity? Perhaps
it lay in the particular ability of Conservative Members to live
beyond their parliamentary means. It became quite possible to
assess the length of tenure of some Tory MPs by the expensive-
ness of their tastes. For them, the glamour of Westminster now
lay primarily in the associated elevation in personal living
standards for themselves and their families. The amassing of
personal wealth had become an accepted and respectable

motive for occupancy of any corner of a Commons bench on the Conservative side.

Nominally parliamentary business, too, was being pursued for personal ends. For example, in recent years all-party parliamentary committees have increased dramatically in number and changed in substance. The all-party single-country groups have become a source of travel tickets at the host government's expense. The trips are so frequent that sometimes the MPs do not even know the name of the country they are in. Called to account on 6 July 1996 by John Humphrys of the BBC *Today* programme, having been seen sunbathing with her husband on a sponsored trip to Malta, Lady Olga Maitland announced that she was the 'vice-chairman of the Anglo-Portuguese parliamentary group and . . . all the other MPs had similar links; and in Port– . . . er, Malta, . . .' She went on to say that trips by members of all-party groups such as this one to Malta stemmed from 'genuinely deep interest in that country'.

All-party single-issue groups have undergone a very new and unchecked infusion of tied funds. Scarcely a group of any substance is not now financed – and probably initiated and organized – by an outside body. This may be a single company or a cluster of commercial interests; or a charitable lobby group playing the same game. This amounts to outside ownership of what used to be gatherings of Members and peers brought together solely to discuss topics of national importance. It is one privatization too far; another is the alleged habit of new Members of using their parliamentary offices to run commercial businesses.

The people of Britain, I felt, were not comfortable with this. I had been concerned about Conservative political morality for several years. In the 1992 general election campaign, I had noticed that many local party canvassers had withheld their customary services. They could not support such a record of broken promises, such an ethos of self-serving opulence; neither could I. My speeches around the country dried up; I could not maintain the fiction that all was well. Even my speeches in the constituency were much reduced and increasingly reflected my own inherited political values rather than those of contemporary colleagues. My three-monthly party letters, circulated with the agent's newsletter to the thousand or so paid-up local party members, became less party political each quarter.

Public reaction to the death in May 1994 of the Labour leader John Smith shone a new light on the depth and breadth of public disillusionment with current Conservative ethics. Tributes poured in from people at all points in the social spectrum, rich and poor, influential figures and individuals speaking on their own behalf, to honour an Opposition leader widely admired and respected for his integrity and honest dealing. All spoke loudly, I believed, of a people hungry for higher standards of political behaviour from the minority they had elected to govern. Swiftly the veneer applied by the Tory spin doctors began to lift and buckle. The 'back to basics' campaign was seen for the fraud it was. A glimpse of what lay beneath it was afforded in July 1994 by the *Sunday Times* 'Cash for Questions' story. This showed the Commons not as a legislature but as a tawdry market-place, a procurer's delight, a den of heaving political corruption. I was reminded of peering into the vast mixer at the rendering company in my constituency and seeing a maelstrom of animals' intestines swirling into a black hole.

While I had some sympathy with my colleagues who needed additional income from extra-parliamentary sources, I thought they should behave in the old-fashioned way and not bring that work into Parliament. It has always been accepted in Britain's political system that Members of Parliament are allowed time to earn an income; but the corollary of that was that the Member gave his or her service to the constituency on a strictly not-for-profit basis. I had always thought that as the electorate paid me, through my parliamentary salary, I owed them the duty of my vote in their interests. In the words of the old adage, he who pays the piper calls the tune. Now, however, the boundary between Members' personal work and their parliamentary work had disintegrated, and with it the primacy of constituents' interests. By the mid-1980s Members saw not the slightest cause for shame in taking complete speeches from a company that sponsored them and pressing the company's case in the Chamber. They could fill their days taking delegations to ministers, arranging paid hospitality within the Palace of Westminster, tabling questions, motions and amendments and setting up informal meetings for their clients. It was no longer possible to distinguish between the tang of commerce and the flavour of genuine debate. Many of my Conservative colleagues could be seen and heard pressing for action of one sort or another on various issues; subsequently it became clear that they were being paid to espouse these causes. The likeable Anthony Steen, another south-west Member, was one of the more pleasant operators, active in support of local and national questions. His entry in the Register of Members' Interests was comprehensive. But what did he really care about, in his heart? The purpose of the House of Commons was to debate issues on their merits, not for financial gain, and this commercialization of business undermined its very *raison d'être*. Money, under the mask of duty, was passing unseen down every corridor of influence as Conservative Members of Parliament assiduously feathered their own nests. In the Thatcher days of huge Conservative majorities Members were given the green light to earn money in any way they wanted; provided they turned up to vote, they could do what they liked. This may explain the explosion in parliamentary questions and ministerial meetings, with all the concomitant expense and delays. Any backbencher seeking an appointment with a minister on a constituency or national matter now has to wait many, many months, however urgent the matter. The parliamentary rent boys have clogged up the works.

Even the Conservative Party Deputy Chairman, Angela Rumbold, could act in a way that seemed to me unacceptable.

One night in 1994 we had both been dining, separately, in the Atrium in Millbank, the restaurant nearest to Parliament. Angela introduced her companion to me and said that he wished to meet me. I was surprised to learn that he had several times requested an appointment with me to discuss a legislative measure then going through Parliament. Angela urged me to see him and listen to his cause, something to do with a Channel Tunnel contract; she had found his case compelling. I questioned her companion as I recalled that someone of that name had called, seeking to see me, from a lobbying company. As I had not wished to be subject to political lobbying I had rejected his approach. Under my questioning he admitted that he was that person. I wanted none of it; Angela continued to press me but I did not give way. The following morning, I learned that she herself was a director of the same lobbying company.

When the people of the United Kingdom elect their Members of Parliament, they believe that their representative will give his or her time fully and with no restraints to their, the constituents', business. They trust you, their MP, to carry in your head, as a knowledge base, the needs of the constituency as well as the interests of the wider community to which the constituents belong. In letters, telephone calls, constituency surgeries, public meetings and face-to-face contacts in streets and shops, in homes and hospitals, they give you their absolute confidence, sharing with you their deepest concerns, their worst anxieties. They know that you have a party affiliation; but they hope, profoundly, that when it really matters you will be strong enough, if necessary, to break those chains, stand up and speak for them.

For most of the twentieth century, MPs received little pay – more a large honorarium than a salary – which only partly covered their political correspondence and telephone bills. My father, for example, used his business secretary and paid for the postage to answer constituents' letters. The House of Commons had no offices for secretaries: Members dictated sitting on hard

benches leading off Central Lobby in the midst of a constant
stream of passers-by. Secretaries were paid personally by
Members and they too saw their job as a calling, a public
service. There were no Members' telephones; all calls were
logged by the switchboard operators and invoiced to individual
Members. Today, the vastly extended Palace of Westminster
incorporates offices for every Member and his or her staff.
Correspondence by letter, fax and voicemail has reached the
proportions of an avalanche. I keep four staff occupied full-
time. The Parliamentary Office costs allowance covers much, if
not all, of that expenditure.

Clearly, changes had to be made to respond to the increase
in business over the decades. But here too, necessary reform was
hijacked by Members who put their own pockets above the
interests of their constituents and Parliament. In 1992 the
Senior Salaries Review Body was tasked with reviewing
Members' pay scales and expenses. I gave evidence myself,
pointing out that coping with a relentless incoming flow of post
was well beyond the physical capacities of a single Member and
one secretary with no office. This was true of many others
besides myself. At one time, for example, both Peter Thurnham
and I had desks in the Cloisters, a thirteenth-century
passageway filled with Conservatives (Labour members worked
on the other side of the courtyard in similar conditions). Night
after night, until well after midnight, Peter would be writing
personal replies by hand, despite having a constituency office
partly financed by himself. For myself, I created a net deficit on
the family budget through personal sponsorship of parliamentary matters. This system cost us a lot of money, but allowed me
time to devote to areas important in my political work, such as
freedom of information and data protection.

Having deliberated, the Senior Salaries Review Body
returned to the Leader of the House, Tony Newton, with significant proposals to raise the MPs' office costs allowance
dramatically but to impose for the first time the kind of

accountability standard in business practice by breaking down the increased sum into discrete elements of expenditure: so much for a computer, so much for a secretary, so much each for other critically necessary office items. There was to be more provision for secretaries' salaries, enabling one and a half or even two people to be employed rather than just one; there was to be a separate personnel office; and there was to be a separate constituency office allowance for each Member.

The Cabinet took one look, jettisoned all the restraints and grabbed the whole sum for MPs' exclusive use, saying: 'The Government consider that the most sensible course is to retain the Office Costs Allowance as a single sum but increase the maximum level.'

I recently bumped into a Conservative parliamentary secretary who wondered 'where it had all gone wrong'. Recalling earlier days when 'we were all so happy together', she had little time for many of today's Members: 'The wrong people are in the House of Commons now. They've spoilt it all. The present Members seem to think only of themselves, and it's true in Central Office too. Members don't behave as they should now. It's the money. Several of my friends have lost their jobs because the entire parliamentary allowance went directly to the wives. And the wives can't do the work. Some of them can't even type. These free university students do all the work, which means it's the constituents who get short-changed.'

If a Member really plays the rules in his own interest, he can secure himself a total annual income of well above £100,000. The parliamentary allowance of £45,000 goes to his wife; then there is the £10,000 allowance for living outside London; then the handsome mileage allowances; and all this is added to the basic salary of £34,000 – which is now going up again, by nearly ten times the inflation rate.

Cases of well-paid wives are well known, and while some of them thoroughly earn their rewards, other cases are less laudable. I know of one where a 'research' allowance appeared simply to follow a Conservative Member's affections as they switched from his wife to his mistress. The public could have been well enough served by this, I suppose, but whatever talents the mistress had in other directions, she showed absolutely no sign of having any training or aptitude for 'research'.

At the same time, then, that MPs are being offered handsome allowances to finance their proper parliamentary business on behalf of their constituents, many are pocketing the maximum amount possible of this official funding and simultaneously diverting their efforts away from their constituents' interests in favour of the causes they are paid to promote by outside clients. If there is a case today – though I doubt it – for the continuance of outside earnings in any form, then transparency must be re-established by the full disclosure of every payment, in cash or in kind. There are not many jobs in which a person can earn two incomes for the same work, or make extra money doing work related to what is being remunerated as a full-time post. Why should the Commons, now filled by full-time, salaried MPs, be any different? The present system, even taking into account the limited measures adopted after the Nolan Report, leads to dishonesty in MPs' self-presentation to the electorate, with Members avoiding their constituents' scrutiny of their activities. Either MPs should earn nothing over and above their parliamentary salary, or should they declare it all and say who has paid it. If the latter course is followed, there should be an absolutely rigid (and rigidly enforced) rule that any Member receiving financial sponsorship, however apparently tangentially related to the topic under discussion, must declare that sponsorship at the beginning of any speech he or she makes in debate. It is no longer enough to say that a financial sponsorship is declared, in full or in part, in the Register of Members' Interests. The Register entries cover so many fields of outside earnings that no one listening to a speaker in the Chamber or in committee can hold all the detail in their head. There should also be a separate list in the Register of all those who receive the parliamentary allowance. At present, only the Fees Office has this information. MPs' family members at least should be publicly listed.

Some of the older Conservative Members feel alienated by the tone of the modern Conservative Party. A hardness of attitude emerged in the mid-1980s which now runs right through the parliamentary party. A new type of career politician has taken over: one who enters the House of Commons as the first step on to a springboard for his or her own financial and other ambitions. The Conservative Party in power has come to be seen as a route not only to social acceptability, as it was in the nineteenth century, but to personal self-aggrandizement: first win a parliamentary seat, then collect some lucrative consultancies, then secure jobs at public expense for members of your family, then – having held some sort of ministerial office – retire to a plum job in the City. Some Members who were carving out such a path for themselves openly begged their colleagues to vote in favour of the Government's position on Nolan and against full disclosure of outside earnings, admitting without a hint of shame that the requirement would affect their income by many thousands of pounds annually.

Behind the scenes, Conservative patronage has grown inexorably. The Chairman of the Committee of Selection, a Government post, has in his gift the chairmanship of and places on select committees, with their extensive foreign travel agenda, as well as on standing committees, where fee-paying consultancies have an interest in many topics under discussion. At the centre of this web of patronage is the Whips' Office; Whips' favourites get seats on the more attractive standing committees (more attractive meaning fewer sittings, or a label that will look impressive to the constituency or consultancy audience). The numbers of the Executive have risen steadily; Government appointees in both Houses now heavily outnumber Commons backbenchers, with eighty-nine ministers, nearly sixty Parliamentary Private Secretaries and twenty-

one Whips, of whom only sixteen ministers and seven Whips sit
in the Lords. The resultant weight of Government on backbench MPs has suffocated constructive disagreement within the
parliamentary party.

The power of the Whips and the power of the consultancy
purse has a most pernicious effect. A backbencher or PPS takes
his customer to see the minister. The company will demand
a result from the meeting: no profitable company pays non-
executive directors or consultants, except for profitable activities.
To achieve this result the Member must behave, in Parliament
and in the party, in a way that is acceptable to the Executive.
Thus the Member is bought twice over: once by the company
and once by the Whips. His political behaviour, including his
attitude towards other colleagues, is moulded by his acceptance
of a fee. He must be a total, unquestioning loyalist. He sacrifices
his only uniqueness to the electorate, his independent judgement. He is another Government hireling.

And the losers in this arrangement? First, the Member's own
constituents; second, the ordinary Members – and therefore
their constituents too – who wish to see the minister on
constituency or national business. They have no bargaining
power, no entry chit to play with; and the Executive therefore
does not bother with them. Even the less formal channels of
communication betwen backbenchers and ministers have
become blocked. The Smoking Room used to be the focal point
for such informal encounters, and the Prime Minister was often
there. Churchill held court in the Smoking Room most
evenings, and Members could approach him directly with their
problems, concerns or suggestions. This never happens now.

It seems as though we have returned to the eighteenth
century, when MPs went to the Commons in open pursuit of
rich pickings for themselves and jobs for their relatives – with
one major, and deleterious, difference: for some years now
the Whips have tolerated, even encouraged, this process in
order to gain a stronger grip on MPs' votes. The younger, less

experienced, less respected Whips of recent years have found it increasingly hard to operate successfully in the traditional way – indeed, have scarcely bothered to try – for reasons I have noted above; in *The Spectator* of 4 May 1996 Bruce Anderson, quoting Tristan Garel-Jones, described the Whips' Office as 'like a signal box during a power failure; you pulled the lever but nothing happened.' Control is now sought via the twin carrots of ministerial office and access to the ear of the Executive for paying clients. Fuelled by bribery and fear, the system appears to work effectively from the Government's point of view; and thus MPs who hire out their services, instead of being the political pariahs they should be, become the Government's most docile and therefore most approved supporters.

It is hard to avoid the conclusion that the pursuit of power for personal gain is all that the modern Conservative Party cares about. And those whose primary political motive is to gain and hold power over others cannot be acting principally for the public good. The ends have finally been destroyed by the continued practice of unethical means.

Chapter 2

A Family Affair

I was born into a Conservative family, yet I did not seek out the party until the mid-1970s. It was then that I came to feel strongly that there was a need to tackle and definitively subdue the dragon of trades union domination then lording it over British industry, national and public bodies and even charitable concerns. That became the party's goal and it became mine also, first as an applicant for a seat and then as a Prospective Parliamentary Candidate.

Of course, I had been steeped in Conservatism from birth. As a family, on both sides, we had been members of the parliamentary Conservative Party since its inception in the eighteenth century, and from late Victorian days nearly every member of the family who had entered either the Commons or the Lords had taken the Conservative whip. I felt obliged to support my family; but it was no hardship to support each of the dozen or so relations who bid to enter Parliament. I saw in every one of them a person who wished to serve his country. I did not feel myself bound to a political party: the tie was familial, not ideological. Throughout my youth I kept my own political reading and thoughts quite separate from the political life of my father, uncles, cousins and their forebears. This separation was the easier for my father's inflexible rule: no politics (or religion) to be discussed at home, lest it lead to family quarrels. Keeping the family together and in harmony was the absolute priority. Moreover, he himself worked so hard outside the home that when he was with us his overriding need was for peace and sleep.

His early morning start to London each Monday gave me, as a small girl, the chance to accompany him to the station, along with my sisters and my beloved mother. This was a great treat. There would be several of my father's colleagues on the platform at Newbury. John Boyd-Carpenter, short, plump and Pickwickian, besuited in black and grey pinstripe, spent the waiting time marching up and down the platform, end to end, ceaselessly. Anthony Hurd and my father would talk together amiably. The Hurds' farmland abutted ours, and after the war the two were joined into a shared Home Farm that sustained both families for thirty years. Eventually the train would come and sweep them all away, bearing them back on Friday evening (Parliament then sat on Friday afternoons). A weary father arrived home in time for supper, a game of chess and then sleep before the Saturday constituency haul, an hour's drive away in Surrey. We often went with him on these trips, which took in surgeries, afternoon fetes, visits to various enterprises and evening branch meetings. Recriminations against the more liberal Conservative policies from local party zealots often meant a late end to these proceedings, and thus an even later return to our quiet West Berkshire house.

Sunday morning meant boiled eggs and church, where my father and Anthony Hurd, as churchwardens, read the lessons. I joined the choir at three and later became the organist, taking my first service at the age of eight. After lunch my father took a long, uninterrupted sleep, either in the garden, with a large silk handkerchief over his face to keep out the light or, with the same bandeau folded and tucked around his eyes, in his armchair in the sitting room, where his recumbent form was framed by pale blue paper-covered *Hansards* lying in stacks on floor and window seats. Sunday evening offered time only for more chess after tea, then supper and bed for a last chance to catch up on sleep before the week ahead. I understood my mother's view that politics broke up family life.

I was not a 'cradle Conservative'. My views did not naturally coincide with those of other family members. For us, the word 'family' meant a large, sprawling, branching organism with roots, offshoots, sprigs and blossomings. It did not mean a tiny island of humanity, two or three people reduced to hugging the notion of family like a comfort blanket. Our family was vast, communicative and knowledgeable, its different members varying hugely in achievement or lack of it, and not averse to criticizing each other. The only link between us all was the tie of blood or marriage. We were a human tribe. That to me, at that time, was what a family was.

My own political ancestors were similarly loosely grouped around unifying themes. In the Lindsay family on my mother's side and in the Nicholson line on my father's there were Conservatives, Liberals and a handful of Liberal or Independent Conservatives. In response to William Gladstone's Wigan speech in 1868, my maternal great-grandfather wrote an early pamphlet entitled *Conservatism: Its Principle, Policy, and Practice*, which displayed the best of contemporary Conservative attitudes within the hierarchical context of his time. At the top of this hierarchy was the deity, seen as the source of the Conservatives' right to rule and duty to lead with humility and compassion.

My mother's family, the Lindsays, had been prominent in the political sphere since the dawn days of the Scottish Parliament: William Lindsay, 18th Earl of Crawford, was its president during the turbulent 1680s. The Earls of Crawford and Balcarres were both diplomats and rebels. In 1320 Sir David Lindsay, Lord of Crawford and 10th Lord Lindsay, signed a letter to Pope John XXII declaring independence for Scotland; he was ambassador to England in 1349 and 1351. Sir Alexander de Lindsay, a supporter of William Wallace and Robert the Bruce who took his seat in the Scottish Parliament in 1308, and Colin Lindsay, 3rd Earl of Balcarres, who repeatedly forfeited eminent positions in London to support the Jacobite rebels in the early eighteenth century (ending up imprisoned at his ancestral home Balcarres by Queen Anne), sacrificed their prospects of political advancement in pursuit of the same goal. Others argued the case for their compatriots as ambassadors to the English court, and as Scottish Representative Peers after the Treaty of Union in 1707. Later in the eighteenth century, many of the Lindsays became Members of Parliament or married into other parliamentary families, establishing a tradition of active participation in public life which was to continue up to the present generation. In the 1820s James Lindsay, 24th Earl of Crawford and MP for Wigan, married the daughter of John Pennington, Baron Muncaster, an ardent reformer and a friend and political collaborator of the great abolitionist William Wilberforce, who said of him: 'I believe you and I are tuned in the same key, as the musicians speak, and that we strike, therefore, in unison.' Another Victorian Lindsay started the British Red Cross. And Robin Balniel, 29th Earl of Crawford and Balcarres, sat in Edward Heath's Cabinet during the 1970s.

My father's family were not far behind. Nicholsons, Hicks Beaches, Portals and other related family members have been MPs since the latter half of the nineteenth century, when my great-grandfather William Nicholson was the Liberal member for Petersfield in Hampshire. Others put in long service under the Conservative banner. My father, Sir Godfrey Nicholson, MP for the Northumberland coal-mining constituency of Morpeth during the early 1930s, created an early piece of welfare legislation in his Workmen's Compensation Act (1925) Amendment Bill. Identifying himself in the House as 'one of those people who refuse to believe that human ingenuity is powerless to lessen the shock caused by the impact of economic catastrophe', he worked hard to bring all sides of the House together, including Isaac Foot, on benefits for miners and their widows. In both respects he exercised a profound influence on my political beliefs. His mother was of Huguenot descent, her family one of many forced to flee France in the seventeenth century when the Protestants' freedom of worship was withdrawn with the repeal of the Edict of Nantes.

My own political and personal ethics grew out of this living heritage and an immensely happy childhood. From both sides of the family I inherited the drive to fight for the weak and the oppressed. My political instincts were not taught; they were inborn. The example of adherence to truth and respect for others set by my parents and teachers framed my life. My parents' moral leadership emerged, unstated, from my observation of their work for others. My father called politics 'the finest form of public service'. My mother chose a more direct route, giving personal and private help to the orphaned, the old, the poor. Absorbing these inherited values, I weighed them against what I read – and I read constantly. Perhaps because I could not hear well (my severe deafness was not identified by any of us until I was nearly seventeen and pursuing a musical career), for the first ten years of my life I relied hugely on books. Anything I could find, I read and pondered over – Victorian, Georgian, Elizabethan, medieval, Roman, ancient Greek, Egyptian or Sumerian: history and literature gave me my world. I learned early on, from Alphonse Daudet's *Lettres de mon Moulin*, that only the writer's own language reflected his real thought, gave us the glimpse of his world that he sought to offer us; the best of translations was only a crude echo, serving as a spur to read the original. Written languages (Latin, Greek, Aramaic) were easier than spoken. I worked and explored alone, reading anything I could lay my hands on. Music was another delight, and was the main reason I went to church. I made friends outside the confines of classroom, age group and social circle with people from the farm and the village. I had a loving, cohesive family, freedom and a secure environment – every child's dream. I was a lucky girl.

It was almost a shame to leave my nursery teacher, Miss Booth, and go away to school, but I begged my parents to let me go when I was only seven, wanting to follow my sisters whom I loved. The next four years I spent on the Sussex coast, where the beach seemed always cold and pebbly and the sea an unforgiving grey. But we had good teachers and small classes, and I did well. Then, at the age of ten or eleven, I moved closer home to a convent school, St Mary's near Wantage, and here my world was clouded when my vision suddenly dimmed. Sadly, the best advice my parents were given stipulated no spectacles and only one hour of reading a day. Nobody was aware of my severe, inborn, hearing deficiency; now, with sight and hearing both blanked off, my world shrank dramatically. The loss was doubly hard because hitherto my eyes had stood in for my ears. It was a tough time then and for long years to come.

Though cut off from much in my immediate environment by these physical barriers, I was still aware of what was going on in the wider world. Certainly the injustice of political life – and some of the less appealing characteristics of the Conservative Party – became clear to me early on. I was at boarding school when Nasser nationalized the Suez Canal Company and Cairo Radio denounced my father as a fascist hyena, in spite of his abstention, notwithstanding a three-line whip, in the vote on the invasion. The Farnham Ladies bayed for my father's political blood. Though he was condemned abroad and attacked at home, I thought at the time that his reasoning was much clearer than that of the Eden 'Empire strike-back' brigade. My father's point was simple: we could not win. And he was right. The trouble is, political revenge is fuelled by failure, and my father was pilloried for being right. Had he been wrong, had the Establishment won their little war, his local Conservatives would have been magnanimous about his 'mistake'. Instead, the threat of deselection sharpened the local meetings. My father hung on, but in Sevenoaks the constituency association passed a vote of no confidence in Nigel Nicolson (no cousin, just a friend) in December 1956 as a result of his declining to support the Government's policy on Suez, and in 1959 he was deselected from his Sevenoaks seat. He never returned to Parliament.

Watching my father's political friends at work in government, I formed a view that the two most essential ingredients of a working government within a mature democracy were compassion and competence. Of course, the Conservative Party had never really had a philosophy as such. Its ethos had been to remain in power as a loose coalition of people from different social backgrounds who shared the view that British society would best be served by gradual, evolutionary change rather than radical reform on theoretical principles. Such a sensible-sounding policy of pragmatism, however, can degenerate into the pursuit of personal wealth and social advancement by party members as readily as a policy of absolute ideological purity. Followed with a less cynical purpose, it enabled Liberals such as Gladstone to serve in a Conservative Cabinet, while an attraction to the underlying values of Liberalism prompted Churchill (who in 1922 argued strenuously for proportional representation for the House of Commons), to take a walk across the floor of the House from the Conservative to the Liberal benches in 1904, steps he did not retrace for twenty-one years. Politically this was a long, long time. There were values in Conservatism then that were seen to work against the tide of personal gain. Only when the disparate strands of Conservativism coincided, with capitalist values and compassion held in balance – not an easy feat – could the Conservative Party straddle the centre ground of politics with a wing on either side.

My father's generation carried grief within them. Some had experienced the end of the First World War as combatants, some as childhood observers. The Second World War came upon them when they were decision-makers. Perhaps already old before their time in the 1930s, they saw their efforts to sustain a peaceful Europe disappear beneath a tide of evil. This and the poverty of the inter-war decades marked them with a sadness tinged with fatalism – but also with a belief that the future must be better. The march of the hungry from Jarrow in 1931 was never forgotten. After 1945 a determination both to eliminate poverty and to resolve armed conflicts by peaceful means crossed all political boundaries.

Much of the shared vision of many of the political leaders and Members of Parliament of that period surely came from their experience in the armed forces in the First and Second World Wars. Thrown together in facing danger and death, they won and accorded mutual respect, and gained a camaraderie and compassion cutting across party and political differences, a sound perspective on what mattered and what didn't set against the slaughter of millions of European people twice in half a century. Wider experience of close contact with all kinds of people from backgrounds different from their own enabled them to understand the problems, difficulties and deprivations the population continued to suffer in the 1950s. Both Selwyn Lloyd QC, a Speaker of the House of Commons, and Enoch Powell had reached the rank of brigadier. Former Lieutenant-Colonel Edward Heath and Denis Healey had been in action. Peter Carrington won a Military Cross for gallantry as a tank commander. I saw Richard Wood, who had had lost both legs in the forces, in great pain answering questions at the Despatch Box. My own grandfather, who after 1918 served as a Conservative Chief Whip and Coalition Cabinet minister, spent much of the First World War as a volunteer, aged forty-three in 1914, in corporal's uniform in the trenches.

As a child I saw poverty in the years after 1945. In the village near our farm at home, farm workers and their wives were my best friends. I saw these women's hands worn almost to the bone through overwork: taking in washing for pay, scrubbing floors, cleaning their own outside lavatories. I wanted to take away their pain. In the constituency I saw the genteel elderly crushed by the anxiety of surviving on inadequate incomes and war widows with pensions counted in sparse shillings. And there were many spinsters: a second twentieth-century generation of young women who had missed the chance of marriage and family life. In London, where I was taken to visit my father at the House of Commons, great areas of the city were still grave reminders of the Blitz. In France, I saw, the story was the same: too few young men and a harshness in the relentless toil of rural life. In French society, too, the yawning gap of status conferred by birth, dividing the chateaux' inhabitants from the ordinary people, remained as wide as ever. I hated that divide wherever I found it. For me, all people were of equal intrinsic value. The necessities for everyone, to enable them to start to develop their natural talents, were obvious: health and education. And simply in order to be able to settle and create families, people needed physical safety and a degree of comfort. I yearned to bring these things about.

For such changes to be brought about, political reform on the grand scale was needed. In today's querulous society, it is difficult to accept the extent to which politicians of all parties agreed on this. Perhaps the socialists expressed it with greater zeal than those on the right, who saw reform less as a mission than as a prerequisite for survival, but it was nonetheless broadly accepted by most that the provision of the population's basic needs was very high on the political agenda. Although I did not see more than a fraction of the national picture, six years of war had left the Britain of 1945 both economically and socially devastated, and with vast debts of gratitude and more to the United States.

Housing was one of the most important post-war imperatives and one of the dearest to my father's heart. It always featured in his speeches. During the war Churchill had embarked on vast plans for reconstruction and recovery when peace came. He wanted millions of prefabricated homes put up swiftly to meet the need. My father had worked hard to secure Churchill the party leadership from which he had led the wartime coalition Government. Our shock and sadness when he lost the 1945 election were profound. Then, as when a Labour Government was returned some years later, I comforted myself with the thought that the new Labour MPs were not enemies: they were

like us, but had different ideas about how to achieve good
things. And yet the downside of these good intentions, in
practice, was only too plain to me. In 1945 the new
Government launched radical reforms: a welfare state, a free
national health service for all, and widespread nationalization of
major industries and services. Our Great Western Railway
gained in anonymity, and lost in staff pride. The 1948 National
Assistance Act repealed the existing poor law, making local
councils responsible for housing the homeless and for providing
welfare services for the physically handicapped. At home, we
felt shocked when many wealthy people switched immediately
to the new, free GP service when they could well have afforded
to pay and stand aside for the poor to claim priority. The
wartime coalition Government had laid the groundwork for
health and education reforms as early as 1942, with Lord
Beveridge's plan for health and insurance, and 1944, with the
landmark Education Act drawn up by Rab Butler, the wartime
education minister and architect of many consensual
Conservative policies. His Act meant that my nursery and
primary teacher, unqualified because of the war, was not
allowed to teach. She was just one among many. Our district,
like others, lost good teachers who could not be replaced. Were
quality and continuity to count for nothing?

The Attlee Government carried through these wartime
plans into its peacetime programme. Attlee chose a Cabinet of
great talent and varied background. His post-war achievements
included granting India her independence, a policy urged on
him by two young MPs whose advance parliamentary delegation reported back to him the views of the Indian people: they
were my father and Arthur (later Lord) Bottomley. Margaret
Thatcher has described Attlee's administration as 'a genuinely
radical and reforming government'. She admired people who
got things done. In Attlee's case this meant confiscating all the
time reserved for Private Members' Bills and using it for
Government business.

Ranged against the Labour benches was Winston Churchill. My father took me into the Members' Smoking Room at an early age to meet him. (Today this would be frowned on.) He was deeply disappointed at his rejection by the electorate, and as prescient as ever. As he had warned against growing Nazi militarism before 1939, so now he preached the same kind of warnings over the Soviet Union. He wanted the United Nations to be a force for unity and action, not 'merely a frothing of words'. As the years passed, Anthony Eden's wooden courtesy was succeeded by Harold Macmillan's diplomacy. I saw how the Conservative Establishment protected itself, to its own impoverishment. Men like Enoch Powell and Iain Macleod, so clearly the odd ones out, remained outside the magic circle, their intellects and passions never really accepted by the insiders. To me it seemed that the dividing line was wrongly drawn. They were silently tarnished by class division, the English bugbear, according exaggerated allegiance to the old school tie and insufficient respect to personal talent and achievement.

In my own education and early career path, I benefited from a very different approach, where acceptance depended on quality of work alone. At first I pursued my music, and at sixteen reached scholarship standard to gain a four-year studentship at the Royal Academy of Music – my hearing loss unknown at the time both to myself and to the Director, Sir Thomas Armstrong. Then, in 1962, my working life started in earnest with entry into ICL by competitive examination. This was not an easy route: I had no maths or science, and the company normally sought a first-class degree in one or the other as a precondition of entry. However, after much persuasion, I sat their eight-hour exam as the odd one out included for personnel sampling purposes, and won through.

I spent the next ten years working with computers. It was a decade of rigorous, constructive thinking, analysis, innovation and project creation; I gained experience of management, and of persuading as well as educating clients. The next step was to pilot, then field test, the new systems. This was work that gave me vital opportunities both to develop my mind and to lay valuable groundwork for the future.

While I was with ICL the company took over Ferranti, which became the jewel in their crown. I had a family link with the new addition: my maternal grandfather had financed the ideas of the founder of Ferranti, first by employing him to install electricity in his large house at Wigan, Haigh Hall – a novelty at the turn of the century – and then by setting him up in a laboratory. The laboratory collapsed and Ferranti went bankrupt; grandfather, undaunted, set him up again. From those small beginnings grew this vast international company, a major player in computer technology in the critical post-war years.

Later on, as ICL struggled to survive, the Government stepped in and took a 25 per cent stake in the company. Subsequently, many of the most innovative people began to leave to set up new companies themselves. They couldn't afford to have their wings clipped intellectually by the iron hand of Government ownership, their imagination stultified by the constraint of distant, ill-formulated Government objectives.

At the request of the Department of Education I and my team (I was put in a management position at twenty-two) worked out an innovative scheme for the computerized marking of schoolchildren's exam results. It was a simple idea and we put it together fast. The unpleasant part came when the Department demanded that we adjust the results to fit prearranged percentages of gainers and losers in the different categories within each exam. We argued back in favour of absolute standards, but relativism – and the power of the customer – won the day.

A vast City of London international insurance scheme cost me nights and days over many months, challenging the computer hardware with an expensive system I had rescued from an over-enthusiastic ICL sales executive. He had sold the largest insurance company in the City a self-design software system that wouldn't work at the price he had contracted. The customer had already paid up half the price and ICL couldn't afford to lose the contract. I managed to redesign it without the customer knowing, fundamentally restructuring the program so that the contract goals could still be reached. It was a tough assignment. Halfway through the impossible happened and I concluded we had equipment failure. This never happened, as the heavily tested American RCA equipment (ICL's manufacturing design skills were badly lacking) was customer-proof: if anything failed, it was the software. And yet, after number-crunching the machine's gigantic memory until it exploded consistently night after night, for six seven-day weeks, I knew that it was the machine, and not my thinking, that was at fault. As a result, every single RCA machine throughout the world (and they had sold hundreds of thousands) had to be expensively modified. My system worked.

My career also gave me a welcome contrast to the semi-public life that I had earlier experienced as a member of a parliamentary family. Family privacy seemed to me to be the burnt offering on the altar of the House of Commons; I felt that it was best to assume from the start that if you had a close family member in Parliament, particularly in the House of Commons, you lived as if your family were open to scrutiny by the public as of right. But although I was now heavily involved in a quite different world, I remained in touch with political life, not least through my father's associates. More than most Members, perhaps, my father always had friends in other parties. George Thomas from Wales, later Speaker of the House of Commons, Arthur Bottomley, Colonial Office Secretary and informally my godfather, Lord Houghton and George Thompson, Member for East Dundee and subsequently EU Commissioner and Liberal Democrat peer, were among them.

In 1964 my work took me to Africa, giving me the chance to exercise my skills in the service of a developing nation as well as to make friends with people in Zambia, Malawi and Zimbabwe (then Southern Rhodesia) on their own ground. Here, too, I learned the reality of colour prejudice. I found at the ball held to celebrate Zambian independence that I and the Zambian minister of finance were the only people dancing together from opposite sides of the colour divide. Others drew back from us. I could not suppress my enjoyment of cultural diversity – the great fascination of humanity – to please negative thinkers. Surely celebration of cultural difference was the real way to value others' lives?

Earlier that year I took time off from designing computer systems in Zambia to go to neighbouring Malawi to celebrate that country's independence, too. I found my father with the frail but inspiring Iain Macleod, George Thompson and another Labour Member, sweating in the African sun: his luggage had gone to Brunei, not via Bulawayo, and his suit was thick blue serge.. It was good to get to know Jo Grimond, whom I had always admired. He found me a small space beside him in the packed, tiny Parliament in Zomba, then Malawi's capital city. Dr Banda, the President, had asked one delegate from each of the member nations of the UN and most had come. The British delegation was led by an uncle of mine, the Lord Chancellor, Lord Dilhorne, formerly Reggie Manningham-Buller, who handed over the Parliamentary Mace. Prince Philip represented the Queen. All sat stoically through six hours of speeches by Dr Banda.

If friendships with members of other parties were acceptable to the Conservative Party at that time, how much more so were friendships between those of different political views within the Conservative Party. Among my father's close associates was Neil Marten, who much later on, as I redrafted my speeches to try to find a seat, was one of my mentors, and whose wife Joan was a member of the Council of the Save the Children Fund. Another close family friend was the great historian Robert Rhodes James, who by the time he became an MP already had a distinguished career to his credit as *chef du cabinet* to the Secretary-General of the United Nations. Earlier, he had been a House of Commons clerk. My father had been his chairman on the Estimates Committee when they wrote the important report on *Government Control over Public Expenditure*. All three of them had different views, Neil differing most profoundly from the other two, perhaps, in his unyielding opposition to the Common Market. But it was entirely accepted by everybody that each should respect the points of view of the others, and that all could talk freely together in the Commons Members' tea room without incurring criticism from within the party.

My own career progressed with a move into management consultancy, one of a tiny handful of women among hundreds of men. My strength lay in the creation of best-quality, long-lasting, low-cost computer software systems, as one of the new breed in the sunrise industry of information technology. By 1969 I was working for John Tyzack & Partners as their computer consultant, a job I took later into another partnership created by three leading City-based chartered accountancy firms, Thompson McLintock, Whinney Murray and Mann Judd. We called ourselves MM&WM for short. One partner with whom I worked closely in both firms, John Cuthbertson, was an accountant, a man much older than myself but with imagination and a truly innovative mind. We worked well together in John Tyzack for some time on projects such as chasing £7 million unaccounted for at Warwick University. With the Government auditors on their heels, we searched and found where it had gone and tightened up their systems. With another partner, this time an engineer, I helped transform a decaying family timber company in the East End of London whose bank overdraft was being called in.

My father left Parliament in 1966, declaring that he was a square peg in a round hole, and he could not represent effectively the views and aspirations of that new young constituency who would vote for the first time in 1969 with the lowering of the voting age to eighteen. His political interests and contacts, however, remained very much alive and his talents were still in demand. The Labour Minister of Health, Dick Crossman, had called him after his retirement and begged him to take on the chairmanship of the St Birinus group of hospitals treating mental health and psychiatric problems, including autism, which was spread throughout Berkshire, Buckinghamshire and Oxfordshire. And it was through his tip that John Cuthbertson and I were invited in 1970 to bid for the contract to work on the local government reform plans of the newly victorious Conservative Government.

Before the 1974 redistribution of responsibilities, local government organization in Britain had been a hotchpotch, patchwork quilt system of elected local councils, a higgledy-piggledy distribution of variegated pockets of power. The tiny county of Rutland had parish pump matters to contend with when compared to the mighty cities such as Liverpool. A decade earlier, Keith Joseph had worked prodigiously on the regionalization of local government. The purpose was clear: the regeneration of the United Kingdom in response to modernization. To him and his colleagues, new methods of communication, vast housing projects and an uninterrupted surge in both population and education standards meant that larger local authorities must be created to wield these larger powers. Labour's return to government in the 1960s destroyed that opportunity; but when the Conservatives regained power in 1970, Keith took the chance immediately. Conservative national politicians respected and wished to strengthen local and regional autonomy, a very different story from today's attitude of suspicion.

And it was Joseph who addressed us when, along with the other bidders, we presented ourselves at the Department. A shy man in public and in private, he declared that local government had to be reformed but gave no reasons, simply outlining the brief curtly. Central government needed to achieve a fundamentally restructured system within the shortest time-scale.

Those present were invited to bid and given just six weeks to submit their proposals. The plan that was chosen would immediately be implemented. The room was filled with people, all calling themselves management consultants; it looked as though the ministry had taken everybody listed 'management consultant' in the telephone directory and invited them all. At that time there was no peer group quality control organization as there is today, and those conferring the title on themselves because it was a catchy American import, or simply because they could find no other job, dragged down the reputations of partnerships such as my own.

John Cuthbertson and I went back to our offices to pull together the most constructive plan we could within the ridiculous time-scale. Our criteria were local accountability, economy of style and maximum effectiveness in communicating both with central government and with the local electorate. It was a task for Goliaths. And our work was wasted. Faced with what must have been a battery of conflicting proposals, Keith Joseph took the easy option and went for an off-the-shelf template proposal, which just weighed up different people and expenditure volumes and similar statistics and pushed them into a predetermined pattern. Within a year or two this was the reform pushed through Parliament. As a result of this surgery, local strengths were drastically weakened while central government gained a simpler and ultimately controllable system which eventually allowed unchecked centralization of local power and cut away the roots of local accountability. A system was put in place which, almost as an inconsequential by-product, started to professionalize local democracy. Such were the demands of time and distance to travel in these new council positions that the out of work and the retired were really the only people who could make themselves available. Later, as an MP in Devon, I discovered why the county councillor from Yelverton was retired: a four- or five-day weekly stint in Exeter and four hours driving daily put the job beyond the reach of anyone in salaried employment. But it also meant that even she could not continue in the end, forced out by sheer physical exhaustion. So much for the Tories' sniping at councillors depending on state benefits: the unemployed became the only source of readily available and willing nominees for local elections.

From pure computer work I moved on to IT with a charitable purpose. In 1973 I joined the Save the Children Fund, first to sort out their computer system, then to work on organizational matters generally and finally to tackle their fund-raising. I looked both wide and deep in my quest for ways to jack up their income fast and economically; the purpose being, of course, not simply to amass money but to expand the charity's work for needy children everywhere.

The work was mainly medical. Listening to the overseas doctors, I learned that they wanted the balance of care to be swung away from disaster relief to long-term preventative work. I cajoled the organization into creating the 'Stop Polio' campaign using the standard vaccine in Malawi, Zambia and Swaziland, and raised £10 million to make it work. To broaden the European base of support I turned to the Netherlands, France, Germany and Scandinavia. After two years' hard work, I had an eminent Dutch board led by the Chairman of Unilever Netherlands, Chairman of Honour Queen Juliana, and a former minister of health as deputy. Through negotiation with the early polio vaccine pioneer Dr Salk and France's leading-edge Merieux Research Institute, Stichting Redt de Kinderen launched full-scale new vaccine trials in French West Africa under WHO monitoring. Collectively, we were saving millions of children from the threat of disability or death. Five years on, sadly, the Save the Children Fund UK discarded the campaign, saying it was too prominent, and absorbed the work into its normal programme. Our eminent epidemiologist Dr Nicholas Ward left for Geneva, rejoined the WHO and now runs the vastly expanded and very successful programme internationally. I stayed on the Dutch board for ten years.

Finally, I led the way with two other senior colleagues to form the new International Save the Children Alliance, based in Geneva. I worked in the United States, Australia and New Zealand to raise funds and make new contacts, and supported Poland's leading child-care organization against US antipathy (nothing the Communists could do was right for them). My only sadness was that after the 1979 general election and on my promotion to Director, Save the Children forced me to cut out politics. As a result, I could not fight the 1983 election; indeed, in the run-up I was in New Zealand, refusing selection by telephone.

My international experiences in the course of this work included the unhappy as well as the rewarding. Late in 1978, attending a huge international child welfare conference in Iran, I left the culminating royal reception in one of the Shah's many palaces. The gulf between him and the people I had seen on the street was more than I could stomach. His courtiers spoke and dressed and behaved like denizens of pre-revolutionary Versailles, and he himself gave me no sense that he knew or cared for his people, who lived at levels so far beneath him. I found I could not accept hospitality from a ruler who spurned his people's needs, and for the first time, as the guest of a foreign government, I repudiated my host, walking out into the Tehran night. It took hours to find my way back to the conference hotel. Several months later the revolution erupted and the Shah fled.

On a more positive note, my continuing international work, particularly within Europe, reinforced my conviction that coordination and cooperation with our near neighbours brought a quantum leap in results, with solutions to apparently intractable problems sometimes generated by novel thinking from a different source.

All this was some way ahead in my first year with the Save the Children Fund, when I was pinned to their London office in Queen Anne's Gate, right by the beauty of St James's Park. Still held on a peppercorn rent from a kindly public landlord, it contained a mix of staff of different ages, backgrounds and traumatic personal histories. Two of the older women, self-effacing and with careworn faces, bore the tattoos of Auschwitz victims. Others were full volunteers. The organization worked at half or less of the speed to which I was accustomed as an IT professional. I accepted this restraint in the cause of helping children, for the time being at least; if I were to stay, I knew, I would want to get them up to speed, but this would take time. Meanwhile, the slow flow of work left me with plenty of time to ponder, an overspill of energy for evening and weekend use, and time to think about politics more seriously. My earlier career in ICL and then with fellow information technology experts had given me what I needed, a full and satisfying professional life which used up most of my time and energy. Any of either commodity left over I had used in social and charitable work, whether for lepers in Africa or street children in London's East End. I had recently spent four months as a volunteer in an orphanage in India. I did not want to do that in the Save the Children Fund; after all, my days were now spent supporting that sort of work. Now, at last, I could dive into the political field. I had the time and the energy, and, most importantly, I was in one place, not racing from pillar to post across the country and across the world to meet clients' needs and sort out their (usually self-made) problems, working five times as hard as the clients themselves in the process.

I had always admired the women in the House of Commons whom I had known. From the physical vastness and kindness of Bessie Braddock through to the sharp wit of Barbara Castle and keen intelligence of Shirley Williams, most had been Labour. I knew that the Conservative Party had not been women-friendly as far as positions of responsibility were concerned. Only the volunteers were welcome, and they were expected to be the beasts of burden, invested with a spurious glamour by glossy titles, bouquets and endless vacant applause.

Chapter 3

'Don't Bother to Try'

Nineteen seventy-four brought two general elections within one year, followed by Ted Heath's loss of the Conservative Party leadership in February 1975. At least, we thought, Labour would be able to control their own supporters from a position of strength in Government; in fact, the weakness of their in-built client relationship with the TUC meant that Downing Street and Westminster were driven from behind. From my vantage point at Save the Children I saw the situation worsen for the poor, who could not buy alternatives to erratic public services. The country seemed to be locked in a fight to the death between bosses and workers, to the long-term detriment of its industrial performance and much else besides.

The trades union movement owned the Labour Party financially. The unions' donations, modest though they were, enabled hundreds of union members to put their names forward for selection as candidates with no fear that they would lose all their income if they entered Parliament. But the efficiency of the movement in seeking fair shares for all in the workplace had led in the post-war years to the exercise of greatly increased worker power in the pursuit of higher employee benefits than businesses could afford while still producing their goods or services at a profit. Admittedly, many British businesses were slow in adapting pre-war management styles to employees' new aspirations. While the Allies were imposing workers' councils in defeated Germany, Britain's bosses slumped back into Edwardian paternalism or worse. To my mind the ethos of the trades union movement was impeccable: brotherhood meant equal respect for others and fair shares for all. But union practices had evolved into a monster that seemed to act without heart or common sense. How could a hospital porter have the medical knowledge which had to be the primary requirement for judging whether or not an operation should be delayed? The undertone of compensating employees for poor treatment by giving the unqualified power over the professionally qualified in the workplace was too strong to ignore. It overrode any normal constraints on behaviour within an organization. Worse, it smacked of the destruction of knowledge, to me the ultimate sin. The infamous phrase 'them and us', implying the existence of an inborn and permanent divide of lifestyle and priorities between worker and boss, re-entered the common vocabulary. The same divide appeared in public and private organizations.

Even in charities, such as Save the Children, which traditionally put service to children at the top of the agenda, huge rifts between staff and volunteers suddenly opened up, and the work for disadvantaged children suffered as employee rights took precedence. In the face of a lack of accountability characteristic of charities (no electorate, few shareholders and only victims as consumers), the innate sense of service mission faltered as social workers fattened their personal portfolios. As I worked on, secondary picketing started to stalk our playgroups like hostile hooded armies appearing on a peaceful skyline.

Grumbling is a negative pursuit. Nevertheless I increasingly found myself guilty of grumbling against the Government. Put up or shut up? The situation, nationally and at work, was too troubling to stay silent. I decided to fight. I telephoned Conservative Central Office and asked how to apply to become a Parliamentary candidate.

A form arrived by post: large, stiff, elegant, as if it were an invitation to apply for membership of the (male-only) Carlton Club. It was printed on cream laid paper, four sides folded into two. The questions were for men: wife's maiden name, her background, her interests. I had no wife. My own family history; full name and title. I hoped that Emma, with no give-away female designation, might be seen as an erudite eccentricity. Four referees were wanted, preferably magistrates and vicars. I put down eight MPs. That filled the wife gap nicely. The final quirk gave the gentlemanly game away, revealing definitively that this invitation only went to those already chosen to take part in the Conservative game. At the foot of the last page, just above a fat space for signature, lay a small black-edged box space half the size of a thumbnail demanding to be filled in. There was just room for a tick or cross in response to the question: 'Do you agree with all Conservative Party policies?'

I paused. It must be a joke. Either that or the ever-shifting policies of the Westminster leadership were really seen as an irrelevance to party functioning and it was the wife's parentage which really mattered. Most likely that was the answer. Lineage, not competence, was the mark of a worthy Conservative candidate, if this job application form was any guide. No one could agree with all the policies of any national political party. No Conservative MP that I knew did. The policies frequently conflicted with each other anyway. One MP would be arguing for public funds to be spent on some project in his constituency while his colleagues argued against it. Despite the weight of party seniority in the Research Department, the general election manifesto sometimes seemed to be almost ignored by MPs and public alike. The Labour Party had an annual conference which was allowed to call its parliamentary leaders to account. In contrast, the Conservative annual conference was like a gargantuan, and very fierce, vicarage tea party. The meeting itself, not the stage-managed debates, was the heart of the event. In the Conservative Party, policy came from above (from Rab Butler, Hugh Fraser and Ian Macleod) and was not questioned by the party faithful.

I had found the words of both Alec Douglas-Home and Edward Heath as party leader inspiring. They expressed views which harmonized with my own, on overseas aid, regional development, housing and the EC. The Conservative manifesto of October 1974 proposed a Speaker's Conference on electoral reform, completing plans already brought forward by the party for strengthening democracy in Scotland and Wales. As for Europe, the Shadow Cabinet claimed – correctly, in my view – that 'by far the most historic achievement of the last Conservative Government was to bring about British entry into the European Community'. I fervently agreed, as also with the view that 'only through unity could the Western European nations recover control over their destiny'. I ticked the box. I did not know all of the party's policies, but I was comfortable with the critical points of the recent manifesto. Nevertheless, the space given for the answer made it a bit of a joke question.

Back went the application form to Conservative Central Office. Then the summons came: I was to be interviewed by the Party Vice-Chairman with responsibility for candidates, a man of eminence and a Member of Parliament. Next, he said, I had to see the Vice-Chairman for Women, Lady Young. Then, depending on what my referees said in their submissions, he would decide whether I could go forward to the Selection Panel.

Lady Young could not have been kinder or more polite. But as a working woman I was astonished by her response. She told me frankly: 'Don't bother to try for Parliament. The Conservative Party doesn't want women in the House of Commons.' She knew from personal experience. She was in the House of Lords because she could not get into the Commons, despite long service in local government in Oxford. I was puzzled and disappointed. Never had my suitability for any of my previous jobs been influenced by my gender. I went to meet and seek advice from another prominent Conservative woman, then an elected member of Greater London Council, Sheila Roberts. She too had tried to become an MP and failed. Her advice to me was the same: 'Don't bother to try,' she said. 'You'll only be disappointed. They don't want women.' I decided that if other women ever asked me these questions I would never give out such a negative message, such a counsel of despair. If we stopped trying we would never succeed.

I was called for an interview by the Selection Panel. I did a great deal of preparation, working out my views on the major issues of the day, which then included secondary picketing by trades unions and the promotion of British industry through a policy of less Government interference but some residual supportive intervention. I also wanted social change. I was particularly eager to improve the lot of children. I wanted better educational facilities for children, and wider opportunity for higher education. I was deeply concerned about the plight of the poor in the United Kingdom. My aim was to speed up social change at home and promote a more successful and influential Britain abroad.

It was a tough interview. Lynda Chalker pointed out that I had had no local government experience. No, I agreed, my full-time career path had so far precluded that. But what about my decade of experience in industry as a computer software expert and as a senior officer in an important charity? Was that not valuable experience for a prospective MP, giving me extensive knowledge of the world at home and abroad? The other MP on the panel agreed, and with his support I succeeded in getting on the Central Office list of Prospective Parliamentary Candidates. With the threat of an early election hanging in the air, I swiftly received a long list of constituencies looking for candidates. As a newcomer I thought I would get no interviews, so I ticked every box. Almost by return of post I was offered interviews in twenty-five seats all over England. I applied for long overdue leave from Save the Children and accepted them all.

The nearest was Hammersmith and Fulham. On the evening before the interview I had dinner with Airey and Diana Neave, old family friends. Airey worked hard to get more women into the House of Commons and was the architect of Margaret Thatcher's triumph over Ted Heath. He was the

Conservative spokesman on Northern Ireland and briefed me extensively. Airey was also a war hero. His book *Flames of Calais* spoke of my uncle, Brigadier Claude Nicholson, aged forty-two in 1940, as 'a true professional and a perfectionist (who remained splendidly calm) when holding the German troops back, thus allowing the bulk of the British expeditionary force to reach Dunkirk'. Churchill, as Airey wrote, 'afterwards . . . found it painful to speak of the sacrifice which Nicholson and his troops were called upon to make. His reference to Nicholson's refusal to surrender in the great speech of 5 June 1940 moved the crowded House of Commons to genuine emotion with [the challenge] to "fight on the beaches".' My uncle died in a German prisoner of war camp. Airey Neave himself subsequently died in the precincts of the House of Commons when an IRA bomb blew up his car. That evening, while Diana was out of earshot, washing up in the kitchen, he told me he would be assassinated. 'They are going to get me, Emma,' he said quietly. 'I don't know when or how, but they are going to get me sometime.' I found it desperately difficult to accept. But he was right.

As I made my speech on Northern Ireland to my interviewers in Hammersmith and Fulham the following evening, the Conservative Association – deeply divided on this issue – almost came to blows across the interview table. Some members stood up and shouted even as I spoke. Next day Conservative Central Office rang up demanding to know: 'Who is this woman and how does she know so much about Northern Ireland?'

For my next interview I sought advice from Peter Walker, who dispensed it along with tea and scones in the Pugin Room between the Commons and the Lords. As a result, in my speech in Brixton I outlined what needed to be done in deprived inner-city areas. The majority of the committee made no attempt to hide their annoyance and hostility, for I had inadvertently pinpointed their neglect and inactivity: they were the local councillors.

In another chilly interview on England's east coast the woman chairman summarily dismissed me on the grounds that the electorate did not want women candidates without husbands. Why was I not married? I could expect no second interview unless I would guarantee to produce at least a fiancé. New to the political interview scenario, I answered that I was unmarried because my boredom threshold was too low. The room rocked with laughter and she dismissed me furiously. A man followed me out, congratulating me on giving the chairman her come-uppance. He was the local party agent. A second woman candidate at the same interview session was rejected by the chairman with the words: 'Electors don't want married women. You should be at home looking after your children.'

I could not change my gender; but I could change my speeches. It wasn't enough. In Birmingham, I was astonished and saddened when the interviewing committee showed clearly that the problems facing ethnic or religious minorities were not a priority for them. My words on tolerance were considered irrelevant. I sought understanding for my relative failure from a close friend outside politics, a man with a double first in economics and law, then a partner in a leading accountancy firm. 'I am not a politician,' he said. 'But I've noticed that my Conservative acquaintances like to have their prejudices confirmed. You are offering innovative solutions to current political problems. That's wrong. Conservatives don't want new ideas. You should make them believe that any thoughts you have are theirs, not yours, although it would be best to drop new ideas completely. That way you'll stand a better chance. But I cannot see why you want to do this peculiar job in the first place. If you want to help society then design more good computer systems – most people can't do that and you can. Or raise more money for the Save the Children Fund. But politics? For the Conservative Party? How dull!'

But I'd made up my mind. For a change I toned down my thoughts and confined myself to recycling statements taken from the newspapers. It worked. I moved up the lists. In one seat, where I was almost successful, the Labour Member kindly wrote my speech for me: he'd rather fight me than the earlier drab candidate, he joked.

Then in 1976 I made my breakthrough: in Blyth, in Labour's north-eastern heartland, with the second largest Labour majority in the country. Many years before, my father had become MP for Morpeth, overturning (on 1930 bound-aries) the largest, having swapped seats with another colleague on the train to Newcastle when he discovered his friend had the more hopeless seat. My grandfather was against his son going into politics and my father, not yet thirty, had found it difficult to tell him that he had won.

My Labour opponent in Blyth was John Ryman. His agent, Mr Mortakis, had earlier been agent to Eddie Milne, whose book *No Shining Knight* exposed the deeply corrupt world of Councillor Dan Smith in the north-east, in which the award of contracts and councillors' votes were inextricably entangled, and lost his membership of the Labour Party as a result. Subsequently, of course, he was proved correct; but it was too late for him by then. Driving up to the constituency in a Mercedes, Ryman would stop at the five-star Gosforth Park Hotel outside the constituency boundary, change cars and clothes and emerge roughly dressed and driving a Mini for the last fifteen minutes of the journey. He had a cottage in the north-west and a horse for hunting. Not wishing this pursuit to become public among the miners of Blyth, when he hurt himself out hunting one day, sustaining cuts to his face and a head injury, he put out a story that he had had a car accident driving north from London.

Ryman's successor, Ronnie Campbell, was a great contrast. A true son of a miner, he practises an upright personal moral code and is a warm-hearted family man. He and I entered Parliament at the same time in 1987; we became close friends and paired on two-line whips. Ronnie learned a good deal about caring for the people of Blyth from studying my father's speeches, and to his great pleasure named him in his maiden speech as his respected political forerunner. Ronnie sacrificed a lifetime's pacifist principles to support his eldest son who, to his great pride, graduated from Lymston as a Royal Marine on the outbreak of the Gulf War. As he flew off to serve, he called his father and told him, 'Back me, Dad, I need you.' As a result, Ronnie walked through the voting lobbies in support of the Gulf War right the way through the conflict.

In Blyth I met some of the most genuine, hard-working men I have ever come across; despite our political differences, they showed me great kindness and friendship. Many of them remembered my father with affection, having been runners for him, delivering leaflets and messages, as children in elections during the 1930s. The miners took me into their working men's clubs, and the management allowed me down the mine. We went down three miles in the lift. My father, who accompanied me, was much impressed by the improvements in pit safety precautions, and recalled the grim conditions in Bates's Colliery in the 1930s which had prompted him to put forward a Bill in Parliament giving the miners and their families sickness and other benefits. It predated similar legislation for other working men and women by at least ten years. He stayed with the deputy manager to return to the surface while I followed the manager and crawled further into the mine on my stomach, my helmet lamp hitting the tunnel roof if I took my chin out of the warm puddles on the floor of the tunnel. Behind me the local reporter who had come with us got claustrophobia and became hysterical. The week before a senior visiting US engineer had had the same problem and had also been dragged out backwards, having first been knocked out by a sedative injection. On the coal face further in, the shearing machines made the gleaming coal peel off, looking soft as butter shavings. We were six miles out under the sea. The next door seam was shut, through flooding, delaying production.

Mines in the United States and other coal-producing countries had much wider seams, where the men could walk upright and keep dry. Britain was in a tough world market. Later, the manager briefed me on world contracts for coal extraction where Britain's hard-won experience could earn high-skill export contracts. The men who extracted the coal had these leading-edge skills; and yet so many of them were losing their jobs. Canvassing in the council estates on midweek afternoons at election time, I could sense the shame of the workless miners. However helpful the offer of jobs through Government assistance might have been, packing talcum powder into tins part-time was regarded as women's work.

Blyth also had a new town, Cramlington, where thousands of houses were being put up swiftly to take the overspill from Newcastle. It changed the whole pattern of the constituency. A sort of Milton Keynes emerged, but without the guiding wisdom of Jock Campbell, the first Chairman of that great project. Cramlington sat uncomfortably beside the single-industry mining villages, its forlorn rows of red-brick houses in a style borrowed from the architecture of southern suburbs scoured by the north-east wind.

A raw priority for Conservatives in Blyth was fighting against a Labour Party which had been found gravely wanting by a significant portion of its own people in terms of political corruption. On top of this came the trauma experienced throughout the mining community of manpower reductions, pit closures, unemployment and shifts of occupation which undermined the previously cohesive way of life. There were other areas of conflict as well: for example between the tenant farmers and their absentee landlords, invariably Conservative bigwigs. The Ridleys' home lay within the constituency, and Nicholas's elder brother and his wife gave me quiet support. They were old-style local eminences of a sort I knew, sensitive to their tenants' or employees' needs. It was immediately clear to me that, although the brothers had a family closeness, Lord Ridley did not support his younger sibling's harsh political views. Yet Nicholas came up at my request and we spent a happy afternoon one Saturday knocking on doors in new, privately owned housing estates. He toned his political message down significantly once he was on home territory and became an energetic and politically supportive older colleague.

The Conservatives in Blyth had had to work out clearly why they supported such an unpopular cause. One older friend told me that it had been made clear to her that her promotion from deputy to head teacher would never come if she didn't join the Labour Party. Ada never changed her allegiance, and she never got the headship; a Labour supporter did. The chairman of the Conservative association was a woman, determined, hard-working and a local councillor. Her goal was to become town mayor, and to do that she had to weave a complex web of social agreements between herself and Labour councillors. Although Conservatives were very dubious, she took to the mayoral task successfully, her life's dream realized. The association president was Dr Brown, the miners' doctor. Dr John, as he was known, though now elderly, was the eternal optimist. He loved his fellow men and women and worked incessantly to give them hope and health, being rewarded with the rare accolade of honorary membership of the NUM for services to the pitmen. Eileen, his wife, was Scottish. We felt we might be cousins and traced back some family connections. She was enchanting, fierce and possessed of such acute political perception that she seemed almost to be gifted with Scottish second sight. I stayed with the Browns while on the election trail.

Another friend, and another elderly man, was Gerald Kelly, who worked the streets with me from council estate to council estate, acting on Mrs Thatcher's first message to me when I went to see her directly after I had been selected as the Prospective Parliamentary Candidate. 'How can I set priorities?' I asked her. 'The constituency has an overdraft, only a handful of members, mostly in their seventies, and a Labour vote the second largest in the country.'

'Try the council estates,' she advised. 'Use Saturday afternoons to go campaigning.' She was warm, friendly, attentive and rather like a teacher. I followed her suggestion and spent hours at a time on most Saturdays for three years pounding the beat in a self-inflicted personal crusade. I spoke of the need to get our country back to work. I pointed out how union power, all-important to the miners, was in so many instances strangling output, which in the long run would damage their members' interests more certainly and more significantly than shedding jobs and subsequently retraining men would do. I met thousands of people whom I liked and valued. Their lives were harsh and difficult, and the outlook for them, viewed in terms of the likely future of mining, bleak. Some gleams of light came from the power station, another export earner like the colliery, and – on a lesser scale, since I was not convinced that they would last – from the new factories set up with Government funding to mop up the unemployed. The roads network was superb, authorized earlier, I believed, by Quintin Hogg, to open up the region for industrial transport. It was a beautiful area. The slag heaps of Wales were later greened by Peter Walker; in Blyth they barely showed in any case.

I raised funds to liquidate the modest overdraft of the Conservative association and established a positive balance to finance the general election. The membership grew. Slowly, we managed to start new branches. I had huge sympathy for the local people's needs. Had I been elected there, I would have found myself fighting my own Conservative Government from inside the House of Commons much sooner. The social needs of the north were just too big to be wiped out or disregarded, and the poor within society at large has had its purchasing power reduced under successive Conservative Governments. This was not the message that I put forward in 1979, nor the message that came out of Central Office, which promised greater wealth for all sections of society if Britain empowered the Conservative Party to tackle the trade union leaders and release their stranglehold over services and production in both public and private hands. In October 1978, in her conference speech at Brighton, Mrs Thatcher gave an implicit promise to the nation of greater social cohesion when she said: 'At home we are a country profoundly ill at ease with ourselves.' John Major held out the same prospect years later with his borrowed goal of 'a nation at ease with itself'. Both leaders' claims that, if elected, they would correct this uncomfortable situation proved false.

Fighting Blyth was very hard work: three and a half years of relentless grind every weekend and throughout all my holidays, while I was still fully stretched by my job. I tried to keep costs right down by lodging for three pounds a night in a bed and breakfast off the High Street with an elderly couple who treated me like their daughter. Even so, by the end, it had cost me seven and a half thousand pounds. My father helped me recover my financial balance. I did not beat Labour as he had done; but this time at least the Conservatives came ahead of the Liberals. For once it was the Liberals, not us, who lost their deposit.

In 1979 and for many years thereafter, Margaret Thatcher conferred a benefit of vast importance in her personal force of energy and determination to galvanize faltering sections of Britain's industrial and professional base to stem the decline in productivity performance. And yet even with this drive behind the enterprise, capacity was never enlarged sufficiently. Automatic ceilings on industrial output had become inbuilt. Under the Thatcher Governments, large parts of the UK workforce did produce a new surge of activity; but the boom was built on borrowed time and money, and North Sea oil. The British tendency to consume rather than produce and market our inventions was not rooted out. Inevitably, less activity meant fewer jobs, a trend exacerbated by the decline in labour-intensive methods and a process I had observed with

anguish throughout my working life. In Africa I had replaced
hand-written ledgers recording Government payments with
software systems to computerize the public sector: the clerks
had lost their jobs. In the United Kingdom, every new
computer system I'd invented and installed successfully had
caused the client organization to shed employees, sometimes in
hundreds or thousands. Of course, there was new employment
associated with the new systems, but most of these jobs were for
the young and very bright, not for those long in post, well established but usually unqualified. More than any other facet of my
working life I'd come to dislike entering a company or
Government department for the first time and meeting the
clerks or shop-floor representatives, aware that my work would
cost them theirs. At least in Save the Children I'd created jobs;
but that was a personal service, not a production industry.
Britain needed exports and the jobs which went with them. As
Mrs Thatcher said at the Brighton Conservative conference in
October 1980, 'Today our country has more than two million
unemployed . . . the level of unemployment today is a human
tragedy.' And I agreed when she continued: 'It is the Labour
Government whose policies are forcing unemployment higher
than it need ever have been.'

Even in Save the Children I felt the rough end of the trades
union movement in the late 1970s. With Jane Reed, then Editor
of *Woman's Own* and now Head of Public Affairs with News
International, and Michael Bukht, then our press officer, now
managing director of Classic FM, I had achieved the loan of
Earls Court for three days to run the world's biggest jumble sale.
We collected twenty-five tonnes of flea-ridden jumble and
painstakingly sorted it, keeping it in the upper levels of the hall
and paying the in-house labour force to bring it down in
batches as the stalls ran out of stock. Twenty-five thousand
people came over the three days; most of the petty thieves in
London turned up on the first day, and I called Chelsea
Barracks urgently to seek Army volunteers to help eject them.

The show was up and rolling when the in-house union struck. On the second day, they wouldn't move our goods, leaving elderly volunteers and my small staff struggling with heavy loads of second-hand clothing. Their strike was nothing to do with us. I made a frantic telephone call to TUC headquarters. Norman Willis, the Deputy General Secretary, raced round and did his best to help; but even so, we lost a critical half day.

This experience set me thinking. It was time to get the trade unions to support Save the Children and not oppose it. I called on George Thomas, Mr Speaker, and at my suggestion – and with the provender given by my father – he hosted a large party at Speaker's House for the TUC General Council, most of whose members came. I overran the TUC official speech time (four minutes instead of three), but they pledged support most generously and carried it through. The Inland Revenue Staff Federation took the lead and their General Secretary became a firm friend.

But the fundamental problem would not be solved by the generosity of individuals, and I supported Mrs Thatcher's political plan, announced by her at Blackpool in October 1979: 'Before the year is out, we shall introduce legislation concerning secret ballots, secondary picketing and the closed shop.'

Chapter 4

Blindfold into Europe

I had three goals in entering political life. The first was social, to curb discrimination on the basis of nationality or gender and give everyone in poverty a chance to lift themselves out of that condition and restore or establish that personal dignity so often degraded by poverty's ugliness. The humiliation of illiteracy, the physical exhaustion produced by unremitting manual labour, the ill health often associated with poor diet, were factors which had to be addressed by society if respect for the individual was to have any meaning.

The responsible creation and use of wealth was my second guiding aim. The Labour goal of levelling down seemed to be the other side of the coin from the worship of all wealth for its own sake: both attitudes credited money with an absolute moral value which it simply doesn't possess. Money is a medium of exchange, a wonderfully fluid enabling device. The honest creation of wealth was of critical importance in order that it could be put to responsible use, preferably both by the individual and by the community; but while the proper use of money was a part of my value system, money itself is value-free. The giving of direct aid to the poorest of the poor was a remedial albeit an essential and continuing action; but it was not a philosophy, merely one means among many of working towards the achievement of equality of opportunity for each and every person.

Thirdly, it was my conviction that the enlargement of knowledge and its dissemination and use for benign purposes *(la culture de la paix)* demanded the creation of a civilized society with high moral values which respected a freedom to explore thoughts, but with no theft of intellectual property – on which, perhaps, should be placed the highest value of all.

Focusing domestically, I saw that the Conservative Party owned, *a priori*, the desire to create wealth (but not, as its later years in government have shown, an equal and permanent commitment to its responsible use by the state), while the drive for social change lay firmly embedded within the philosophies and practices of both Labour and the Liberals. I believed, wrongly, that those social principles would gradually be taken more explicitly into the Conservative portfolio of beliefs to make it the real centre party of our political age.

As I studied the serious writers and listened to the politicians I saw that the concept of the European Community could or perhaps already did embrace these personal ideals. The Cabinet had agreed on 27 July 1961 to apply to join. Heath was then working under Macmillan as the leader of the delegation charged with conducting the negotiations. I had had a considerable respect for the wily grey fox, Harold Macmillan, but to me he represented the older generation; Ted Heath, the future. Macmillan had concentrated on shedding the Empire Britain had once ruled, while Heath was building the new links and interconnections that would forge an empire of people freely exchanging goods and knowledge, and, motivated by their common desire to escape the bitter past, building a peaceful, multinational culture. My life was to be dedicated to helping in some way to achieve those goals. Heath offered the political philosophy and framework that opened up my path.

The European path, of course, was one which was to remain closed to Britain for some time. De Gaulle's first veto of Britain's proposed membership was made on 14 January 1963 and formally announced on 29 January 1963 by Couve de Murville – in prescient terms, perhaps: 'We want to make a European Europe!' De Gaulle's second veto was delivered on 16 May 1967. Finally, in 1971, Edward Heath signed the Treaty of Accession. It was also a path fiercely contested, both before and after that date. Indeed, the issue of Europe has caused more intra-party strife in these years than any other. The strands of argument about first one commitment and then another have led, like slow-burning fuses, to charges of varying force. First the Conservative and then the Labour Party have been torn apart by internal contradiction.

And yet the history of Britain's involvement in the European project seems to be characterized by a wilful obfuscation by successive Governments of its true nature. The first White Paper ever produced on Community membership was published in the summer of 1962 by Macmillan's Conservative Government. By far the most important one, in the light of subsequent events, was that on *Legal and Constitutional Implications of United Kingdom Membership of the European Communities*, issued by the Wilson Labour Government in May 1967. Two other documents of great interest were published in July 1967 and June 1970; these are the texts of statements made by two Foreign Secretaries of different parties (George Brown and Anthony Barber), speaking to continental audiences and stating unequivocally that Britain accepted the Communities' objectives. No one could reasonably claim that the core information was unavailable or that the important points were not made early on; but plenty subsequently did exactly that.

A. J. P. Taylor famously asserted that the causes of the Second World War received insufficient attention in the post-war years because it was convenient to blame the entire conflict on one man, Hitler, who was thankfully dead. Whether that criticism holds good for academic analysis or not, it does not do justice to the seriousness with which the advocates of a new form of European integration approached their subject in the 1940s. The European treaties which emerged after the war were formed in response not to Hitler himself, but to his breeding ground: those social, political and economic forces which had proved powerful enough to enslave so much of our continent.

As A. J. Toynbee argued, in 1931, even before Hitler became Chancellor,

> Class-warfare and economic nationalism were cramping the supple movements of an economic system which require a free hand for ability in a world-wide field in order to work effectively. At the same time, political nationalism and race-feeling were making it more and more difficult to organise and ensure the universal peace which the economic world order required for its political framework. In general, the peoples and the countries of the world were disintegrating into an ever larger number of ever smaller and ever less harmonious fragments in an age when technical progress was ever more insistently demanding that all major social operations should be conducted on a world-wide scale.

In 1933, on the day after Japan attacked Manchuria, the British Government decided to abandon the Gold Standard. There followed a shocking spiral of protectionism and poverty which undermined the efficacy and credibility of political and monetary systems alike. Like some peculiarly destructive typhoon, the crisis eventually sucked the sympathies of just enough German voters in Hitler's direction to make the world-wide spread of 'political violence' inevitable.

Some early drafts of a new European order were made in prison by victims of fascism well before the war was won. It is clear from these writings that the timidity of the League of Nations cast a long shadow. Efforts to avoid future wars in Europe had to be ambitious if they were to have any chance of success. Small nations could not stand alone. Protectionism and discrimination on the basis of nationality had to be outlawed. There had to be monetary stability and freedom of movement of people as well as of goods and capital. Competition had to be free and fair. Integration had to embody political, economic and social purposes. Power exercised at an international level had to be subject to both democratic and judicial control. A study commission under the chairmanship of de Gasperi in 1943 made the point that 'National societies must renounce the right to take justice into their own hands and must recognise a jurisdiction possessing sufficient means to settle peacefully the conflicts that are bound to arise . . . The League of Nations failed owing to the inadequacy of its institutions and powers.' Above all, it was no good tinkering around with the symptoms of conflict. The League of Nations and the great powers had expended years of fruitless debate on methods of dispute resolution. It was necessary to address the root causes of war and to do so in a manner which was more likely to endure than anything which had been attempted before.

One contrast between 1945 and 1918 was the emphasis which was placed upon international action after the second war. Altiero Spinelli rightly predicted in 1941–2 that 'The problem of an international order would be seen as superior to that of national order, in a way that was certainly not felt after the last war.' It was not that nationalism had escaped criticism during the Great War. Franz Brentano, for example, had had the courage to write in 1916, in 'Epicurus and the War': 'How absurd it is to suppose that it is better for a whole people to be robbed of its happiness and to be subjected to unspeakable suffering than it is for the state to fail to maintain itself in full power or even to cease to extend its power. This species of madness, which is all too common at the present time, contains a most peculiar reversal of the proper order of means and end.'

The problem was that this criticism had failed to find adequate practical expression after 1918. The founders of the new Europe which emerged after 1945 were clearly and consciously determined that the same mistake would not be made again.

This determination did not suddenly spring from nowhere to descend, fully clothed, in the Treaties of Paris and Rome. It appeared in various forms in a number of treaties and agreements well before then. The Treaty of Brussels of 1948, for example, which Britain signed and which has normally been seen as primarily concerned with defence, actually ranged widely across 'economic, social and cultural collaboration', as its title suggests. Article I began with this paragraph:

> Convinced of the close community of their interests and of the necessity of uniting in order to promote the economic recovery of Europe, the High Contracting Parties will so organize and co-ordinate their economic activities as to produce the best possible results, by the elimination of conflict in their economic policies, the co-ordination of production and the development of commercial exchanges.

Article II added the following commitment:

> The High Contracting Parties will make every effort in common, both by direct consultation and in specialised agencies, to promote the attainment of a higher standard of living by their peoples and to develop on corresponding lines the social and other related services of their countries. The High Contracting Parties will consult with the object of achieving the earliest possible application of recommendations of immediate practical interest relating to social matters.

And this treaty was signed for Britain not only by the ambassador in Brussels, Sir George Rendell, but by the Foreign Secretary, Ernest Bevin, and King George himself.

In some respects this treaty, foreshadowing the Treaty of Paris, which created the European Coal and Steel Community, was more ambitious and idealistic, especially in the sphere of social policy, than the Treaty of Rome which followed in 1957.

Even so, the resolution agreed by the ministers of foreign affairs of the ECSC member states at Messina in June 1955 was ambitious enough to foreshadow the 1993 'working time' directive which was adopted, against cries of foul play from the Conservative Party, nearly four decades later. The Messina resolution stated: 'As far as the social field is concerned, the six Governments consider it imperative to study the progressive harmonisation of the regulations now in force in the various countries, especially those relating to working hours, payment for over-time (night-work, work on Sundays and public holidays) . . .'

The view that peace could not be secured by economic measures alone was clearly understood and widely shared from the very beginning. In 1956, the International Labour Organization reviewed progress towards European integration and described 'the conviction that the ultimate objective of economic cooperation is to strengthen Europe's social framework and the stability of its social and political institutions'. To this end it was argued that 'deliberate steps should be taken to ensure that the benefits of higher productivity resulting from closer economic cooperation will be reflected in improved living and working conditions'. And the third preamble of the 1957 Treaty of Rome, which brought the European Economic Community into being, showed the signatories 'affirming, as the essential objective of their efforts, the constant improvements of the living and working conditions of their peoples'.

Of course, the inclusion of such provisions in a treaty establishing a common market does not derive simply from a sense of social responsibility. The new European partners had bitter and recent experience of the effect of competitive deflation on the social and political fabric of Europe before the Second World War. And indeed, on many points, and especially on matters of discrimination, there were good grounds for thinking that the treaty was too feeble.

The essence of the European treaties we signed in 1971 was that free movement of goods, people and capital comes at a price if it is to come at all. No government could subsequently honestly claim to seek to keep Britain within the European Community/Union while implicitly persuading the British people that first one part of the bill and then another was an affront to our national integrity. For example, the area of 'working conditions', which has proved so controversial in recent years, especially within the context of the Social Chapter, is not a new concern of the EU, let alone one smuggled in by some kind of subterfuge. Action in this field has always formed part of our legal obligations as a member state, albeit a much less important part than would be the case if Britain signed the Social Chapter. (The enactment of legislation on 'working conditions' by qualified majority vote was introduced in the Social Chapter of the Maastricht Treaty, more properly called 'The Agreement on Social Policy Concluded between the Member States of the European Community with the Exception of the United Kingdom'.) We did not join a Community which was devoid of social purpose or even primarily inspired by economic considerations. When Chancellor Kohl marked the ILO's 75th anniversary with an essay entitled 'International Social Policy is the Guarantee of Peace', he was reaffirming one of the central assumptions upon which European integration has been built as well as serving Germany's immediate economic interest.

The founding treaties were not acts of stealth. They reflected the attitude of the time and the approach to dispute prevention and resolution within and between nations which was developed during the war years, not least in Britain. That attitude found its most elaborate expression in the organization of West Germany during the period of its occupation, in which Britain played a highly influential part. Consensus was not seen in the way in which Lady Thatcher has characterized it, as the abandonment of principles; it was seen as an essential defence against the loss of social cohesion described so vividly by Toynbee in 1931.

As the Foreign Office and Cabinet papers of the period show, successive British Governments understood the Community's breadth of purpose very well. Britain's failure to grasp the opportunity to lead Europe in the post-war period represented a failure of diplomacy and political imagination, rather than of intelligence. It was a failure doomed to multiply once Britain actually considered joining the Community.

But what did the British people really know? I recall the early years of Britain's membership very well. I do not recall a single Government-sponsored statement which set out to describe fully, and with candour, the Community's objectives in the social field or the role of the European Court of Justice. There was some peripheral discussion of social issues. I remember some heated debates about migration based on an unwarranted fear that hordes of European workers might want to subject themselves to the rigours of the British labour market. Yet Governments of both complexions greeted questions based on total ignorance with barely suppressed sighs of relief. Fears that the EC would abolish the health service or hopes that our membership might be a step on the road to World Government gave ministers little trouble at the Despatch Box. Governments of both parties got away with characterizing the Community as an economic enterprise. Its political purpose was drawn solely in Cold War terms. Its social and other objectives and the reality of its legal framework were successfully prevented from impinging upon the public mind.

In 1960, in connection with Britain's first application to join the Community, the Lord Chancellor, Lord Kilmuir, was asked by Ted Heath to assess the constitutional implications of Britain becoming a party to the Treaty of Rome. Lord Kilmuir highlighted the implications for the position of Parliament, future treaty-making powers and the independence of the courts. Of the first, Lord Kilmuir wrote: 'Parliament would have to transfer to the Council, or other appropriate organ of the Community, its substantive powers of legislating over the whole of a very important field.' Of the second, he warned: 'To confer a sovereign state's treaty-making powers on an international organisation is the first step on the road which leads by way of confederation to the fully federal state.' Of the third, he pointed out: 'There is no precedent for our final appellate tribunal being required to refer questions of law (even in a limited field) to another court and . . . to accept that court's decision.' His overall conclusion contained counsel which was not the less wise for being ignored:

> I must emphasise that in my view the surrenders of sovereignty involved are serious ones and I think that, as a matter of practical politics, it will not be easy to persuade Parliament or the public to accept them. I am sure that it would be a great mistake to under-estimate the force of the objections to them. But these objections ought to be brought out into the open now because, if we attempt to gloss over them at this stage, those who are opposed to the whole idea of our joining the Community will certainly seize on them with more damaging effect later on.

None of his assessment was made public.

The 1971 White Paper *The United Kingdom and the European Communities* (Cmnd 4715) was Parliament's main source of information from the Government prior to the passage of the European Communities Bill. It stated: 'At present the Communities' institutions are purely economic . . . Certain provisions of the treaties and instruments made under them, concerned with economic, commercial and closely related matters, will be included in our law.' In this, the Heath Government made no advance on the assessment contained in the 1967 (Labour) White Paper, *Legal and Constitutional Implications of United Kingdom Membership of the European Communities* (Cmnd 3301). This played down the question of 'direct effect' of European law. It said: 'Most of the Community law having direct internal effect . . . does not touch citizens in their private capacities,' and drew on the statement given by the Lord Chancellor, Lord Gardiner, to the House of Lords on 8 May 1967:

> May I say that I entirely agree with an observation made by . . . Lord Dilhorne . . . on August 2 1962 . . . I venture to suggest that the vast majority of men and women in this country will never directly feel the impact of the Community-made law at all. In the conduct of their daily affairs they will have no need to have any regard to any of the provisions of that law; nor are they at all ever likely to be affected by an administrative action of one of the Community institutions.

When asked to provide an 'up-to-date' version of Labour's White Paper in December 1970, the Attorney-General replied: 'The general conclusions drawn in the White Paper have not been invalidated in any way by developments since 1967.'

European case law assumed an insignificant role in parliamentary debates about Britain's membership, though cases worthy of mention had certainly been decided. In the 1964 case *Costa* v. *ENEL*, the European Court had stated that: 'By contrast with ordinary international treaties, the EEC Treaty has created its own legal system which, on the entry into force of the Treaty, became an integral part of the legal systems of the Member States and which their courts are bound to apply.' This case was cited in 1971 in *Blackburn* v. *Attorney-General*, but Mr Blackburn's efforts to prevent the signature of the Treaty of Rome were unproductive. In rejecting his case, the Master of the Rolls delivered a judgment which indicated that the judiciary chose not to explore in advance the overriding nature of the EC rules that were about to come into effect: 'It is elementary that these courts take no notice of treaties as such.

We take no notice of treaties until they are embodied in laws enacted by Parliament, and then only to the extent that Parliament tells us.'

The treaties themselves were not well known. When the occupants of the Government Front Bench were challenged on 20 January 1972 'to say that they have read these documents [the treaties] and understood them', a deafening silence followed. On the following day, Arthur Lewis MP said of the Treaty of Accession, 'It is non-existent so far as the House is concerned . . . Yesterday I asked one of the leading members of the Cabinet who said that he had not yet seen it.'

The Treaty of Accession was signed before it was made available to Parliament. When Labour challenged this procedure – for less than noble reasons, it has to be said – the Government tried arguing that it followed a long-established series of precedents. By the end of the debate, when it was clear that this line had proved unconvincing, the Solicitor-General, Geoffrey Howe, simply stated: 'The conclusion is that governments decide, upon the political background of the case, whether treaties are published before signature.' The Commons rejected Labour's attempt to force publication of the treaties. Margaret Thatcher, Cecil Parkinson, Norman Tebbit, Nicholas Ridley, Nicholas Winterton and Kenneth Baker, among others, voted with the Government.

Government statements made in advance of Britain's accession were strewn with examples of different things being said to different audiences about the significance of the undertaking and the importance of its underlying objectives, as set out in the preambles to the treaties. Invariably, the information given to Parliament played down the extent to which any change would be brought about in Britain, especially any change introduced without any further decisive involvement of Parliament.

One of the masters of manipulation was Harold Wilson. At times he seemed wholly ignorant of the Communities' structure. For example, he said in the House of Commons on 10 November 1966: 'I do not think we have ever contemplated . . . that discussions about the EEC meant a European Parliament . . . This is not what we are talking about, and there is no provision for [this] in the Treaty of Rome.' At other times his technique was more sophisticated. He managed to base a hairpin turn in policy upon a chilling premise: that the terms of our legal obligations could simply be overlooked. Commending to the House the Government's decision to apply to join the Community, he said, first, 'Every aspect of the Treaty of Rome itself, of decisions taken subsequent to its signature, and all the implications and consequences which might be expected to flow from British entry, have been examined in depth,' and then, 'In so many aspects of vital importance to this House the actual working [of the Community] is a great deal more relaxed than the wording of the regulations might suggest.' The same line of reasoning was deployed to damaging effect in the Conservative Government's White Paper of 1971 on the subject of the veto. It said: 'The practical working of the Community accordingly reflects the reality that sovereign Governments are represented round the table. On a question where a Government considers that vital national interests are involved it is established that the decision should be unanimous.'

The founding members of the Community understood the treaties very well and they doubted Britain's ability to absorb the enormity of her decision to accede to them. The danger clearly existed that Britain's membership might be based upon either a series of fundamental misunderstandings or a fraudulent determination to persuade her people that little would change and her partners that huge changes would be embraced with enthusiasm. British ministers, both Labour and Conservative, understood their prospective partners well enough to make repeated statements – to European audiences, of course – designed to dispel such fears. Foreign Secretaries George Brown in 1967 and Anthony Barber in 1970 addressed the matter in very similar terms. Compare 'We shall be accepting precisely the same treaty aims and obligations in letter and spirit as yourselves' (Brown) with 'What matters – to you and to us – is that our objectives are the same, and we no less than you will want the institutions to match those objectives. I have said that we accept the Treaties and their objectives' (Barber). The reaction, especially among Conservative MPs, to subsequent decisions and opinions of the European Court of Justice which have referred to fundamental principles of the treaties suggests otherwise.

In a landmark decision in 1976 (*Gabrielle Defrenne* v. *Sabena (No. 1)*), the Court said of Article 119 of the Treaty of Rome, dealing with equal pay: 'This provision forms part of the social objectives of the Community, which is not merely an economic union, but is at the same time intended, by common action, to ensure social progress and seek the constant improvement of the living and working conditions of their peoples, as is emphasised in the preamble to the Treaty.' Many subsequent decisions of the ECJ and of the British courts affecting the rights and interests of employees have followed this logic. Most have drawn outraged opprobrium from Conservative zealots, always keen to accuse other member states and European institutions of betrayal.

Ted Heath's Government cannot be defended by arguing that the objectives of the treaties were dismissed as unimportant because the preambles to them do not form a sufficient basis for the enactment of legislation. His Government was sufficiently aware of the breadth of the Communities' 'objects' to insert a reference to them in clause 2.2 of the European Communities Bill. William Whitelaw, as Lord President, was asked by the Joint Committee on Delegated Legislation in 1972, 'Is [the reference to the Communities' objects] so wide that one can no longer scrutinise with a view to determining whether or not a proper use is being made of the powers given? Is not this saying that in fact you can do anything you like through the power to make subordinate legislation?' He ducked the question completely on the grounds that he would not wish to make an error in advance of his colleagues' presentation of the Government's case during debates on the Bill. Not surprisingly, perhaps, the Committee's final report included a reference to the view of the Donoughmore Committee, appointed in 1929, that, 'Legislative powers are freely delegated by Parliament without the members of the two Houses fully realising what is being done.'

The provision of information prior to the 1975 referendum, notwithstanding the distribution of a case against membership at Government expense, followed a by now familiar pattern: almost complete silence on the interpretation and enforcement of Community law and the social objectives of the treaties.

Britain's immediate and continuing difficulties with Europe, therefore, sprang from a conscious and deliberate desire on the part of successive Governments to obscure the nature of our European obligations from the outset. In the case of the Government of 1970–4, it is clear, from his own much later statements, that Ted Heath did not consider a more open policy practicable. The end, membership, justified the means, economy with the truth. For Labour, the need for some semblance of party unity took precedence over whatever desire for openness might have existed. The arguments of the opponents of membership did include some penetrating analyses of the nature of the obligations involved. Minds as fine as those of Hugh Gaitskell and Enoch Powell were not employed in vain. However, all of us outside the magic circle, both at the time and later, would have benefited from a much wider understanding of the nature of Britain's membership from its advocates, and especially its advocates in Government.

Taken as a whole, the treaties were not unambiguous. The extent to which their wider objectives would be met indirectly by the functioning of a common market, rather than by Community expenditure or by the adoption of legislation, could not be predicted simply by reading their texts. But I can find no Government-sponsored assessment of membership made for domestic consumption which pointed out the full scope of the Community's objectives and policies or the inter- pretative methods of the European Court. Information was seldom readily volunteered. The various White Papers represent compendia of the subjects upon which successive Governments had come under pressure. If Parliament did not know enough to apply pressure over particular subject areas, nothing was said which might encourage further enquiry. During the periods of negotiation and renegotiation, the more penetrating enquiries from MPs were stonewalled on the basis that anything more illuminating would damage Britain's negotiating position. Both Parliament and the press focused on the process of negotiation rather than on the nature of the Communities and the obliga- tions of membership; given that the obligations were sizeable and the scope for negotiation very limited, this seriously distorted the entire debate.

When Margaret Thatcher took over the leadership of the Conservative Party from Edward Heath she made no effort to dissolve the secrecy and transform the electorate, after the refer- endum, into a fully EC-knowledgeable people. Nor did she fully involve Parliament either, perhaps unwittingly helping to fulfil Anthony Sampson's warning of 1971 in his *New Anatomy of Britain*: 'If Parliament is really to be a credible forum for the British problems of the future, it cannot afford to become a gathering of windbags without substance. It needs not only to make much closer contact with the base; but also to grapple with the real sources of economic and foreign policy, which lie outside the frontiers of Britain.'

Yet despite Heath's failure to communicate fully with the public on the European issue, the offer he made in *Action Not Words*, the 1966 manifesto, of 'a Government team which means what it says and knows what it intends to do . . . a Government that doesn't run away; an honest government', still rang true. In contrast, Margaret Thatcher, while professing to support the various EC draft obligations and pushing them through Parliament, in fact was hiding from nearly everyone her secret views.

Mrs Thatcher's first words to the party at her inaugural conference in Blackpool aligned her firmly with advocacy of Britain's accession to the Treaty of Rome as she declared: 'I know you will understand the humility I feel at following in the footsteps of great men like . . . Edward Heath, who successfully led the Party to victory in 1970 and brilliantly led the nation into Europe in 1973.' It is impossible to guess from her more recent statements how much she knew then of the nature of Community membership. Perhaps she was genuinely ignorant of the treaty which she agreed at the time should be signed even before it was made available to Parliament?

How could we have anticipated during her early days as party leader the sort of heated, private exchanges on Europe which she was to have with her senior colleagues? Lord Cockfield was one target. I remember feeling disconcerted by the totally undeserved abuse which was aimed at him from within the Conservative Party during his period as a European Commissioner. In his outstanding book *The European Union: Creating the Single Market* (1994) he has recalled an astonishing conversation with Mrs Thatcher about the Treaty of Rome. She had insisted that action to approximate VAT rates was outwith the terms of the treaty. The following conversation ensued:

Lord Cockfield: It was in the Treaty of Rome.
The PM: It was not.
Lord Cockfield: It was.
The PM: It was not.
Lord Cockfield: It was.

An official was despatched to fetch a copy of the relevant article.

Lord Cockfield: You should have read it before you signed it.

The PM: I didn't sign it.

Lord Cockfield: I know you didn't. But you were a member of the Cabinet which did sign it.

Silence.

In 1977 Mrs Thatcher even quoted Kipling in expressing her support for the ideals of the Community; and she constantly called on Churchill's statements as justification for her own support for European integration. Unless one was very close to her and she let her guard drop, which must have happened sometimes, it would have been impossible to detect hostility towards the EC, or fear of Germany in particular – later to become a very damaging feature of her European policy stance – in any of her public utterances as leader of the Opposition.

Mrs Thatcher's, and subsequently John Major's, treatment of British membership of the European Community and later Union deserves much fuller treatment than is possible in this short book. Nevertheless, it is worth noting here that, even as late as 1987 the party campaign handbook, known as the 'Blue Bible' and produced by the Conservative Research Department, criticized the Labour Party for its opposition to British membership of the EC in the 1960s and lauded Harold Macmillan's efforts to get British admission accepted by de Gaulle. Although British Governments in the 1950s, says the Blue Bible, 'felt some reluctance about embarking upon a course as ambitious and integrationist as that implied by the Rome Treaties . . . by the late 1950s it was apparent that in the post-colonial age Britain needed both a new political focus for her international relations and free access to a large and stable market for her goods.' A following section lambasted the earlier Labour Government for calling for renegotiation of Britain's terms of membership in 1974. It commented that the 1975 referendum result 'vindicated the consistent policy of the Conservative

Party in taking Britain into the Community'. Labour adminis-
trations, it went on, 'could only play an obstructive role in the
Community', and it accused the Labour Party of 'a divided and
contradictory approach [whose] policy has swung back and
forth between outright opposition to the Community and sour
acquiescence in membership' and of attempting to 'turn the
clock back'. By way of contrast, Conservative achievements
since 1979 are listed on page after page, along with exhortations
on the continuing work 'still to be done before the Community
could fulfil its original aims'. These aims are earlier restated as
being those of the original EEC Treaty, in which the founder
members declared themselves to be 'determined to lay the
foundations of an ever closer union among the peoples of
Europe'. And yet in 1988 a booklet entitled *Fifty Questions and
Answers on the European Community*, issued by Conservative Central
Office, denied that 'completion of the Single Market by 1992'
was 'synonymous with . . . a surrender of our independence,
sovereignty or national identity'.

It is hardly surprising that, with all the pressures of a
demanding and satisfying career, as well as work as a party
volunteer, I – along with so many others – believed Mrs
Thatcher supported the European ideal. Only very recently
have some of those closest to her disclosed their own astonishment when they discovered her profound loathing of Europe. A
very senior Conservative has said privately to me: 'Mrs
Thatcher hated Europe. But she hid it perfectly. In 1979, in a
private conversation, she said she loathed it. It was astonishing
how well she hid it.'

Chapter 5

Smith Square in the Thatcher Years

My chance to work with Mrs Thatcher came most unexpectedly with a telephone call in 1983 from the Conservative Party Chairman, Cecil Parkinson. Would I be Vice-Chairman with special responsibility for women? The Prime Minister, he explained, wanted a younger, working woman: I fitted the bill as I had experience of leading large groups of volunteers.

Hitherto my only contact with the party hierarchy had been a fleeting one: a five-minute meeting with the Conservative Party Treasurer, Alastair McAlpine, in which he had asked me if it were possible to use computers to set the current speeches of Labour figures alongside their earlier remarks at the touch of a button. I was, however, already well acquainted with Conservative Central Office at 32 Smith Square. The staff in Number Ten Downing Street said that when Margaret Thatcher first entered as Prime Minister in 1979 it was 'like a breath of fresh air'. The same had been true in CCO when she became leader in 1975. The Smith Square team then was a happy one. Some of the senior staff (the all-important agents) were trained, but the rest were members of political families, who, in return for low pay, got a sense of public service and had fun too. The building, a fine Georgian edifice, was pleasantly shabby inside and the furniture was tatty; but the staff were content, and their enthusiasm made volunteers welcome. The efficient and cheerful George Green, who later worked for me in the House of Commons, was responsible for general office security, stationery, the staff canteen and the telephonists, and for liaising with the party leader's office in the Commons.

The leader's private office was staffed by Caroline Stephens (who later married the Chief Whip, Richard Ryder), Susan Shields, Derek Howe, Matthew Parris and Susanna Burr. (Matthew, later renowned as the *Times* political diarist, rescued a drowning dog from the Thames.)

At this time security, both at Conservative Central Office and at Labour headquarters opposite, was minimal. At 32 Smith Square the staff were mainly part-time or ex-army. There were no security passes, no body or baggage searches and no vehicle inspections. A security barrier to the underground car park was installed after the IRA car-bombing campaign started in 1972–3, but that was the extent of any visible security measures until 1979–80, when a professional security company was brought in and security passes introduced. Until then CCO was run like a family firm.

By the time I became Party Vice-Chairman, a rich Conservative supporter had paid for large-scale modernization of the building. Carpets stretched from wall to wall; heavy folding partitions had been installed to make different-sized meeting rooms; vending machines had replaced the tea ladies with their morning and afternoon tea trollies; uniformed guards monitored comings and goings. All this transformed the party headquarters from the focus of a grass-roots organization to a minor model of a US Republican Party State Headquarters. It helped in staging press conferences, but lost in the 'human touch' stakes.

As Party Vice-Chairman I was able to see at first hand the work of several Party Chairmen. Margaret Thatcher changed the type of person occupying this post. Before her arrival, it had been filled by an eminent, respected political figure nearing the end of his career, sometimes in the Lords, with no axe to grind. Lord Thorneycroft was a good example. When he retired Mrs Thatcher broke the mould and appointed the first of a series of younger, more overtly energetic men, MPs still aiming for the zenith of their careers. In doing so she changed the balance of obligations of the Party Chairman. The new incumbents wanted to put their talents and energies into carving out a successful personal career path, and that conflicted with the Chairman's role of helping others succeed and creating a flourishing voluntary and professional organization. They also demanded high pay, to make up for perceived lost political opportunities.

The post of Party Chairman swiftly became a graveyard. After Cecil Parkinson came John Selwyn Gummer, who was demolished in short order by the press for pomposity. He was followed by Norman Tebbit, who hid himself from view while at Central Office. I worked for all three. Afterwards Kenneth Baker promoted the poll tax and Peter Brooke sacked staff in a destructive purge. Jeremy Hanley was demolished by party and press alike. It was an unhappy decade.

It is revealing to consider that if the Tory Party had been a trade union, its methods of self-governance would have been made illegal several times over by Conservative legislation. Sackings without proper notice periods were commonplace. My most senior member of staff, a single woman, was dispensed with after years of loyal service just as she approached retirement age, thereby wiping out her pension entitlements. What was good enough for the collective voice of the Labour movement was not good enough for our own supporters. The Tory Party's association of democratic reforms with its ideological opponents made it clear that it saw in them a destructive, rather than a constructive, power.

In the Conservative Women's National Committee the atmosphere was strikingly different. Here I found perceptive, energetic women with their ears close to the political ground. I saw it as my job to convey upwards within the party the valuable intelligence which they fed in from their canvassing work and local contacts. Fortunes are now spent on 'qualitative' opinion polling which, for all its scientific pretensions, cannot possibly produce all the benefits of a nationwide network of volunteers to whom appropriate attention is paid. I was fortunate, perhaps, to be at Smith Square when the party, as well as the pollsters, could still get a proper hearing. These were the people in the Conservative Party who experienced in their own families as well as in their towns and villages the bleakness of youth unemployment, the higher bills for children at university. When canvassing they saw beyond the doorway into the poverty of households with no books, just a blaring television spewing out horrors to keep the children occupied. There were some feminists; curiously, perhaps, mostly among the older women, who had fought hard to try to create equal opportunity for women within a Conservative Party inherently hostile to their aims. They hadn't given up; I admired those women greatly.

In Central Office I built upon a system that I inherited from Lady Young. I forwarded the most interesting or strongly held women's views to the appropriate ministers, as well as to Numbers Ten and Eleven Downing Street. We settled into a tight working routine, with working parties looking critically at issues that affected women and families and putting forward realistic, and sometimes unpalatable, views to ministers. We issued press releases, held conferences, and did our best to keep ministers fed with real knowledge about the way their measures were affecting Britain's population.

As Vice-Chairman for Women I spent a lot of time with Margaret Thatcher. Every few months I saw her by myself, with only her Private Secretary, Stephen Sherborne, present, to discuss issues associated with women. Although I was a volunteer, I treated the meetings in a professional manner in order not to take up the Prime Minister's time unnecessarily. I sent forward papers for her to study, up to twenty pages long, setting out points for discussion and reasoning to support my conclusions. These were put in her overnight box by Stephen Sherborne the day before our meetings. She studied the paperwork and, of course, had many of her own ideas. It was both challenging and constructive to work with her, and I enjoyed our time together; on nearly every occasion we were able to achieve some small but significant gains.

With the Prime Minister's agreement, I took the entire 100-strong CWNC to lunch at Number Ten. We brought in caterers and serving staff, and picked up the bill, so that there could be neither any misuse of Government hospitality funds nor any improper crossing of boundaries for staff.

My first suggestion to Mrs Thatcher as Vice-Chairman for Women had been that perhaps the women's organization should not exist at all. In a world where women worked, did we really need a separate group? Would she object if I explored this point? She would not. When it came to discussing organizational changes, she was very open-minded. On other matters it was more difficult for us to reach agreement. She was not keen on independent taxation for women, for example. This seemed to me to be essential. It was something the Conservative women had been working on since 1979. It had even been supported by Geoffrey Howe when he was Chancellor of the Exchequer. The monetary implications of the question for the Government were relatively small, and for non-working married women it meant a very great deal. They would finally be treated as grown-ups by society. Why didn't Mrs Thatcher like it? She saw no gain in it for her party or for her government; and it would cost the Exchequer a small sum of money. She couldn't see any point in a measure that would both cost money and – in her view – gain no extra votes. The equal opportunity aspect of the matter did not seem to weigh with her at all, as I pointed out to her. Her philosophy was all to do with gaining more electoral support. But Nigel Lawson had applied his mind to the problem and was not going to turn back.

I developed a very great respect for Nigel Lawson, and for Peter Cropper, his political adviser at the Treasury and earlier head of the Conservative Research Department. Later, Peter was particularly sad when the Government cut down SERPS, the scheme for second pensions which, if sustained at its earlier value, would have made so much difference to lower and middle-ranking earners. Both Peter and Nigel were fair-minded men and, along with others such as Geoffrey Howe and Douglas Hurd, were seen to meet the highest standards in public service. Maybe Mrs Thatcher's weakness was that she was seen to be acting too specifically in the interest of the party and not sufficiently for the broader good. Even worse has been the rise of so many MPs and ministers who are clearly in it for themselves. The difference is vast and profound.

Nigel Lawson won the argument over independent taxation for married women, and Mrs Thatcher was not very happy with me as a consequence. She only really felt comfortable with people if she could count on their agreement on everything. That was what gave her confidence that she was fully safe. I didn't know what she felt so insecure about. Maybe I failed to recognize how far she had come to get to where she was, and therefore how much she had to lose. I think she believed that she had entered an Establishment of which she was not actually a member. Some parts of it she tried to destroy, partly for her own political safety, but other parts she sought to cultivate. In fact, the Establishment was changing, chameleon-like (as it always has done to ensure its own survival), in response to the transformation of societies and markets; and the Establishment she ended up mirroring so successfully was itself an image, not the real thing, which had moved on. The former senior BBC World Service correspondent Harold Briley offers an interesting perspective on Mrs Thatcher from the previous decade:

> My own experience of Thatcher, whom I saw every week as a lobby correspondent in the secret, so-called 'Blue Mantle' meetings when she was leader of the Opposition, was of an arrogant person (though she told me more than once how compassionate she really was!) who would not listen, indeed would not let other people

get a word in. What always interested me was how what were at first her weaknesses – lack of knowledge of foreign affairs – grew into her greatest strength: 'world stateswoman', etc., and her strengths, which were home affairs, especially the economy, proved to be her weakness, in the mess her economic policies left for Major.

The 1980s also saw the IRA inflict significant damage on both Margaret Thatcher's Government and the Conservative Party. The loss of Airey Neave in 1979 had been both personally devastating for the Prime Minister and catastrophic for the way in which she made up her Cabinet. The assassination of Ian Gow in 1990 was another desperate personal blow and deprived her of a most knowledgeable adviser on Northern Ireland. The blowing up of the Imperial Hotel, Brighton, in 1984, aimed as it was against her personally, her close friends and key members of her party, affected political life profoundly. It resulted in the creation of an ever-present ring of steel around all the most senior Government figures; links between Mrs Thatcher and ordinary people were cut and communication between Government and society at large became subtly different, and less effective.

Take the annual Conservative party conferences. Since the Brighton bomb, delegates cannot move freely. Securicor, the national and local police, and Special Branch are all on duty. Two conferences later, there were still ships on the horizon, helicopters in the air, armed marksmen on the roofs. People can no longer touch and speak to their political leaders easily. Now those leaders base their understanding of public attitudes on polling statistics and the *Daily Mail*, rather than on direct contact with ordinary people. Perhaps it was the IRA which lost Mrs Thatcher her keen political sensitivity, her ability to keep her finger on the pulse.

The personal trauma inflicted by the Brighton bomb, of

course, was intense. I noticed a number of people suffering extraordinary stress which in some cases went on for a very long time indeed. For at least a year afterwards, people told me that they woke up at the time of the bomb, night after night. One woman had been found by the firemen three hours after the bomb had exploded, sitting on the side of her bed in her nightgown, staring at the floor. As the bomb went off she had sat up and swung her legs out of bed to get up as an automatic reflex: in a state of shock, she stayed there for hours, not knowing what she was doing. My own enduring memories are still of John Wakeham's beautiful and lovely wife laughing with him at breakfast that morning in the Imperial Hotel. I looked back as I left the room and happened to catch sight of her joy and happiness at their shared domestic merriment. Sixteen hours later she was dead. And of Anthony Berry, walking down the circular stairs past me and out happily into the fresh night air at 1.30 a.m. with a small dog on a lead, cheerfully responding to teasing comments from the rest of us sitting around after the Conference Ball.

When the blast struck I was asleep, a few doors along from Mrs Thatcher's suite. Diana Neave was also in the Imperial Hotel the night the Brighton bomb went off. Like me, she escaped unscathed. She told me afterwards that the only time they had stayed at the Imperial Hotel, Airey had gone out of his way to find and show her where the fire escape was, telling her that sometime she would need it. He had never done this in any other hotel, at any time in their married life. She thought of him as she went down it to safety in October 1984.

*

The breadth of thinking displayed by Conservative women in the mid-1980s was not a new phenomenon. The 49th Annual Conservative Women's Conference of 1978 had concentrated on family matters and had put forward many generously

motivated motions – albeit mixed in with a long list of calls for
the return of the death sentence, minimum sentences, stricter
sentences, corporal punishment and stronger penalties that
would allow 'the punishment to fit the crime'. Those expressing
more moderate views included ministers and other senior
figures, such as Christopher Tugendhat, then a member of the
European Commission. The balance was always struck by the
collective views of the shadow ministers themselves, who
seemed to offer a greater tolerance combined with challenges to
the Labour Government to bring in a freer market. It was easily
possible for people such as myself to support the party while
disagreeing profoundly with a number of views that individuals
or groups expressed. Shadow ministers and many MPs clearly
did so.

When I set up the women's 'high flyers' conferences, Mrs
Thatcher came and spoke; she was particularly successful at my
first Asian women's conference. Her message was always
positive, since, as she had declared before she became Prime
Minister, in her party conference speech at Brighton in 1976,
her strategies stemmed 'from a clear, coherent political philosophy'. In that same speech, she had declared that 'for the
Conservative Party, politics has always been about something
more than gaining power. It has been about serving the nation.'
Her own goal was declared in another conference speech, at
Brighton in 1980, as 'the restoration of Britain's place in the
world', and although at Blackpool in 1981 she emphasized
'friendship with America', she nonetheless constantly reaffirmed
her Government's support for the European ideal. The EC was
a central and accepted theme at the women's conferences.
Margaret Thatcher's photograph appeared on the Women's
Committee's Annual Conference programme of 1982 beneath a
statement of the theme 'Living with our neighbours, particularly
in the European Community'. Baroness Young, as Vice-
Chairman, commented that with these neighbours 'we share a
common heritage'. It was even possible to believe that Mrs

Thatcher's earlier statements on child care and nursery education were sincerely meant; her picture on the frontispiece
showed her with a baby in a crèche. The British Section of the
European Union of Women was gaining in stature. By 1990
virtually all of those women agreed that for the sake of 'living
with our neighbours', their rallying call in 1982, their woman
Prime Minister should go.

As Party Vice-Chairman I worked as a volunteer in Central
Office, personally financing my office furniture and most of my
modest expenses. Between the two elections of 1983 and 1987 I
visited every constituency in the United Kingdom. Perhaps the
funniest incident of the entire period, which should have shown
me how fixated on class judgement the Conservative Party
remained, came at the end of a day spent touring in the Home
Counties where, nursed by an energetic agent, Tony Garrett –
by 1995 the senior agent in Central Office – I spoke at nine
events over a wide area, driven between them by Tony. To keep
ourselves up to the mark I suggested I should deliver a different
speech at every one, which gave Tony the chance to offer
constructive criticism between stops. We kept ourselves alert
with friendly banter and arrived a little late at our final event, a
dinner at which I was to be the main speaker. It was dusk, and
we were weary and less than bandbox to look at when we
turned into the gravel driveway of a large house. We knocked at
the door. No answer, but a good deal of convivial noise from
behind it. We knocked again, more loudly. Steps approached
and the door opened, to reveal our hostess. She scrutinized us
carefully, looking me up and down, and came to a swift conclusion. 'The tradesmen's entrance is round at the side,' she said
briskly, 'that's where you go.' The door closed. I leaned against
the pillar, weak with laughter. Would the Conservatives never
drop their outdated obsession with class?

Nineteen-eighty-six was a peak year of work for the CNWC.
By the time of that year's conference I had already visited fifty-
two constituencies, all in my spare time. I had also chaired a

conference of party officers at St Hilda's College, Oxford, to discuss priorities, and a mid-year conference at Brandon Hall Hotel, where Alan Howarth MP was a speaker, together with a clutch of local councillors. One working party published a report on financial provision for maternity, another studied the Warnock Report and a third researched material for a publication about the work of women in the Conservative Party. We had four all-day meetings addressed respectively by Michael Heseltine, Kenneth Clarke, Baroness Young and Peter Walker, and the General Purposes Committee had met on four other occasions. I had had regular private meetings with the Prime Minister, creating important organizational and campaigning material to be discussed on each occasion. I met the Party Chairman frequently and was planning a younger women's conference later in the year as the culmination of an under-35s recruiting campaign I had launched the year before. There were now ninety women on the candidates list, a splendid increase on the days when I had become a candidate in 1976 as one of eight. We were a force for good, a balanced, friendly group.

And yet, despite all this energy, palpable dedication and productive activity, the CNWC continued to suffer from the Conservative Party's core attitude towards its female members. This showed especially in the pitifully small numbers of women carrying the Conservative banner in Parliament. An early Conservative woman MP was elected in 1922; there were three in the Parliaments of 1923, 1924 and 1929; then 1931 saw a heady leap, with thirteen Conservative women returned. After that, the numbers shrank, to nine in 1938 and just one in the great post-war election of 1945. There were six in 1950–1, ten in 1955, twelve in 1959; then the numbers started to go down again, to eleven and seven in 1964 and 1966. The peak was reached in 1970 with no fewer than fifteen, but the advance was not sustained. The two elections of 1974 produced nine and seven, that of 1979 eight. Even in 1983 just thirteen

Conservative women MPs were elected. Meanwhile, on the other side of the House, Shirley Williams had broken the Labour mould with three important colleagues.

Had the Conservative Party really wished it, the pattern could have been changed. The Conservative Party is now, and has been for a long, long time, an army led from the top. The leader rules the roost. He or she controls both the political and the financial aspects of the party's internal organization. The leader has the resources of Central Office at his or her disposal through the power to appoint the Party Chairman and Deputy or Vice-Chairmen – of which there many be any number or none, as the leader's whim dictates. The Party Treasurer also reports direct to the leader, who has the authority to disclose or withhold party accounts and the names of donors. No leader ever has chosen to opt for disclosure; fund-raising remains a secretive business. When I was in Smith Square in the mid-1980s the Treasurer's Department did everything in secret: even the secretaries were sworn to confidentiality and all the papers and ledgers, including the reference books and files, could be seen by Treasury staff only. Everyone else – including directors of other departments and the most senior agent of the whole party organization – was kept in the dark. The Prime Minister, as party leader, was heavily involved in party fund-raising, as John Major has been. This left open the worrying possibility that considerable sums might be donated by less than scrupulous businessmen seeking to use this means to get themselves in line for highly profitable Government contracts. I was particularly concerned about possible overseas sources of funding. Very considerable efforts by some party volunteers, who made themselves very unpopular in the process, to persuade the party to publish full accounts, were to no avail.

Much is made of the autonomy of the local Conservative associations, but even this is not all it seems. Certainly the various associations around the country appoint their own agents; but what this means is that the richer constituencies get the better ones and the poorer constituencies get those least well suited to the job or, more likely, no one at all. In the post-war years many agents came straight out of the services, with records of bravery and distinction and an ideal of public service. In today's Conservative Party, personal advancement is an almost respectable motivation. And there are plenty of mechanisms by which the much-vaunted local autonomy can be overridden. The party leader holds sway on most issues in most constituencies. Exceptions only prove the rule.

At party conferences, for example, the placing of motions and amendments with constituencies by the leader, or senior ministers, or their special advisers, via senior officers of the National Union ensures that the line approved by the centre takes priority. Even after John Major's arrival at Number Ten, manipulation of the process of passing resolutions and amendments remained the order of the day. In 1992, in the immediate aftermath of Black Wednesday, there was great anxiety about the prospects for debates in which Europe would figure, especially those on foreign affairs and the economy. The traditional self-congratulatory foreign policy resolution had amendments tabled to it late in the day, but any real concern about the outcome was misplaced: for while the amendment which was passed appeared to come from a constituency association, in fact it had been drafted with the assistance of Douglas Hurd's special advisers, and was handed to an association with an approved speaker to move it.

Given the party's military-type structure and chain of command, it would have been simplicity itself to organize a higher intake of women – and of ethnic minorities – into the House of Commons. The first step that was required was a significant strengthening of the candidates list to incorporate the many excellent women who applied. This happened slowly and gently over the time that I was Party Vice-Chairman, with the very considerable assistance of the effort put in by my fellow

Vice-Chairman, Tom Arnold MP. But the constituency associations who did the interviewing somehow got the message,
heavily endorsed by the Agents' Association, that women in
even small numbers would not be welcome. I was reminded of
a senior partner in a City accountancy firm who openly
admitted to me that if he were to recruit on merit, female
trainees would outnumber males within a very few years,
because the quality of female graduates trying to enter
chartered accountancy was so high. He deliberately held them
back because, as he put it, he did not wish to change the
complexion within the offices of his clients. It was rather like
that in the Conservative Party.

Nor was there any way forward by means of a wider appeal
to the broader membership of the Conservative Party at selection stage. When it was known that an MP would be retiring or
a sitting Member had died, the candidates list was brought out
and the local association chairman, together with his agent and
perhaps another volunteer, were brought up to London to go
over it carefully with the Party Vice-Chairman for candidates.
Of course, they were free to do as they wished; but they were
guided towards pre-set choices. Thus at the very least Central
Office could ensure that the long-list which the constituency
then drew up would include the Central Office plums, the fruits
Smith Square wished to place in Parliament to flavour the brew
one way or another. Latterly, there has been a distinct bias to
the right, especially on prospective candidates' attitudes towards
Europe.

The constituency chairman would take this long-list back to
his selection committee, a small group put together rapidly out
of the larger association committee and numbering from six to
ten. They drew up a short-list for interview. That list was
whittled down and then a larger committee, numbering fifteen
to twenty people, would interview the surviving applicants. For
the final selection the committee would enlarge once more. This
expansion of the selecting body lent an illusory air of breadth to

the process: for at each successive stage, in order to pass to the next and larger board, the would-be candidate had to please very few people indeed. He or she became expert at making an instant appraisal on walking through the door, and learned to stand before these small groups of activists and size up the most likely prejudices of the most significant individuals while the inevitable pleasantries were being exchanged. My suggestion of US-style primaries which would give the full membership equal rights in the selection process was laughed aside.

Once the old system of careful selection for the Central Office list by two Members of Parliament, an agent and only one volunteer was replaced by the notorious weekend cockfights, the influx of greedy politicians, now so familiar from the Conservative benches, inevitably followed, with almost the lowest common denominator coming through. Would-be entrants from business and the professions give up in disgust. Yet we need non-political background experience very badly in the House of Commons. Instead we get proponents of views shaped not in the world of real work, but in the often sterile and low-quality debates of the Oxford Union or the Federation of Conservative Students – the latter a body which, during the 1980s, sank to such depths in harshness of attitude and standards of behaviour that even Central Office could not accept their pronouncements on social issues and disbanded them.

A new type of would-be candidate began to appear in Central Office and the Research Department, straight out of university, where they had read some politics-related subject. The more aggressive among them immediately got their heads down and fought unscrupulous battles for political preferment, their first objective being appointment as special adviser to a minister. These were relatively new and highly paid political posts, funded by the Civil Service but existing outside its rules of impartiality and its other terms and conditions. Now numbering thirty-nine, on salaries of over £70,000, they emerged in order that ministers could be supplied with political input – euphemistically termed 'political balance' – rather than relying on impartial advice and information from civil servants. Their weekly meetings were chaired by the head of the Conservative Research Department. The huge attraction of appointment as a special adviser for the politically ambitious is the chance it offers to get close to the scent of real power very early in one's career. The disadvantage is that there is no security of employment whatsoever. These advisers rely utterly upon the continued approval of their ministers. Those who do not please, or who fail to make the next step on the political ladder, either fade away or move into some more rewarding, less artificial environment than politics. Once ensconced with a minister, however, the key objective is to find a seat and there-fore to court approval by adherence to the fashionable Government line of the day. Equipped with the knowledge they acquire at their minister's elbow, they can make the 'right' points, having developed that special brand of cunning which accompanies the fierce pursuit of personal ambition at an early age.

Candidates who come into the party the old-fashioned way, by taking time out of non-political lives, are at a hopeless disad-vantage alongside these professional young turks. Too many special advisers never even have to fight a hopeless seat. Not for them the years of persistence required to gain selection even for a marginal; not for them the mixed good fortune of selection for a by-election, where failure can, and usually does, mean instant political death, having shouldered all the blame for defeat. For candidates who have not been professional politi-cians from their early twenties, it can take five years (for men) or ten years (for women) of fighting, getting selected elsewhere and fighting again, before having any real chance of entering Parliament. For many women even ten or more years of effort can produce no result at all. Yet those prepared to go the distance gained the beat-pounding, door-knocking knowledge of a locality equalled only by policemen and vicars and, if worked with a will, sensitivity and a ready ear, the insight, at least from time to time, of a probation officer or a social worker. When candidates coming through that route finally made it to the House of Commons, they arrived with a grounding in political reality and an ear cocked to listen to the electorate.

The contrast with the new breed coming in by the fast track was very stark indeed. Somehow, along the line, Thatcher's parliamentary children misplaced their hearts. The struggle to get in fast and rise swiftly to catch the leader's eye was so acute that the idea of serving the wider public interest never really impinged upon them. So keenly was this change of ethos felt by some older Members that, for example, Sir Anthony Grant, a former Vice-Chairman for candidates, said in his farewell interview in *The House Magazine* in March 1996 that he would not recommend anyone he knew these days to go into the House of Commons since they would find their colleagues were unacceptable as friends. 'I don't like the look of the next Parliament one little bit,' he said. 'I think it is going to be full of party political "full-time" horrors.' Similarly, Douglas Hurd, former Foreign Secretary, has put on public record that he was very unhappy with the unfriendly new breed of Tory MPs. The contrast between many of today's Members and the Conservatives of the 'godly society' to which my great-grand-father's generation belonged, where a perceived right to govern was matched by a corresponding obligation to do so properly and in pursuit of right values, could not be starker.

The Conservative Research Department was converted during the Thatcher years from a forum for thinking from first principles into a compliant generator of propaganda – another mechanism of central control. As a recipient of countless Research Department briefs, I can testify to the declining quality of thought, which seemed to gather pace after the third election victory in 1987. Loss of originality was progressively accompanied by increases in inaccuracy. The whole party, like the leader, was being treated to non-stop accompaniments of easy listening. Best of all were the short synopses of in-house opinion polls, endlessly inventive in their striving to prove that black was white.

'Research' within the party was also increasingly hampered by the growing factionalism of this period. Placemen and women of the right within the Research Department and Central Office and among the ministerial special advisers achieved critical mass before Margaret Thatcher left office. Once a sufficient number of sufficiently senior positions were controlled by right-wingers, the process became self-perpetuating. It also threw up curious results from time to time as some senior ministers of centrist or centre-left sympathies seemed wholly ignorant of the extent to which they were now surrounded by ideologues. For example, strenuous efforts were made before the 1992 election to ensure that doubt could be cast on the extent to which ratification of the Maastricht Treaty could be held to be a clear manifesto commitment. The text of the manifesto itself praised the Maastricht Treaty as a success, but at no point did it commit the Government to ratification – although to those not aware of the Research Department's avoidance strategy it would have been very difficult to pinpoint this. Looked at the other way round, however, it would have been intellectually unsustainable to argue against ratification on the basis of this manifesto. Thus lack of adequate leadership resulted in the creation of an illusory statement.

Barren of new ideas and infected by an excess of factionalism, the party came to promote the medium above the message. The huge success of the 1979 election campaign has lived long in the party's memory. The new techniques of political communication used then, like the policies promoted, had been developed in opposition; again like the policies, since 1979 they have undergone endless refinement but no fundamental re-examination. The essence of these techniques is cynicism – a cynicism that has permeated the thinking of ministers and their advisers so thoroughly that it is no longer a source of hesitation, let alone shame.

*

Fortunately, during my time as Party Vice-Chairman, I could find substantial support for my views on such matters as poverty and discrimination among the Conservative women. Take the conference of 1986 again. The Women's Committee of South Thanet called for an increase in social services in the south-eastern area in order to assist the unemployed and the rapidly growing number of elderly, retired and disabled people, together with students and elderly and disabled visitors. They called for responsible research into the causes of infertility because of their concern for the distress this caused to both women and men. Chichester deplored the unequal treatment by the DHSS of married women as opposed to married men in the blatantly discriminatory refusal to allow them to claim invalid care allowance. In my own speech, I raised applause when I declared that 'when there is unfairness in society, when natural justice has not yet prevailed, we must use all our energy to put the matter right. We do care for the truly unfortunate, we aim for balance and fairness for all.' Nobody jumped up to object when I added that we had to work 'with a regard for truth'; and Lord Whitelaw, answering the debate, did not disagree.

But this breadth of view was increasingly alien to the new, hardline mainstream of the Conservative Party. Later that year I attended the TUC annual conference in Brighton. (At the start I walked up to the platform to greet those I knew; they begged me to back off, lest I be identified as Conservative Party Vice-Chairman and their credibility suffer accordingly.) I went up to the top of the hall and sat down in a seat in the gallery. A man came and sat beside me and whispered in my ear. I moved away. He followed me and sat down again and whispered once more. Irritated by this badgering, I moved again. He followed, leaned over me and said: 'Miss Nicholson, Miss Nicholson, I am the only other Conservative in this place and you won't even say hello.' Only two Conservatives at Britain's foremost labour market conference? The division between the Conservative Party and the trades union movement seemed complete.

Once a year, at the Conservative party conference, I held a lunch for Mrs Thatcher with the higher-ranking women with the voluntary party organization. I ran it formally, so that everyone was introduced and had a chance to speak. This was inevitably a somewhat tense affair, given that the space we found in her diary was always the day before her own conference speech. Naturally, everyone else wanted the Prime Minister's time too; but I fought hard to keep this slot for the women's organization, with her full cooperation, and it paid dividends in boosting enthusiasm and support.

Sadly, however, my efforts as Vice-Chairman for Women were nullified after I left. Ironically, this came about in part because of a rift between the Conservative Women's National Committee and the party's women MPs over the question of abortion. The CWNC sent out a press release taking a liberal line on the issue (as they were entitled to do); some women MPs objected to its tone. The Party Chairman, Peter Brooke, decreed that CWNC could no longer issue independent publicity; it was forbidden to send out any press releases not vetted by the Chairman's Office and completely in line with party policy. The women's organization shrank. The high-fliers' conferences I had started for women of excellence, irrespective of whether they were card-carrying Conservatives, were changed: only those who already belonged to the party could be invited, and those who came had to pay. I felt that this would exclude so many women that sponsorship from industry should be sought. My conferences had been free.

The broad horizons of the women's organization narrowed, numbers dwindled rapidly, and noises of deep unhappiness began to filter through to me in a continuing stream of lament.

Once more these loyal women were being reduced to the performance of supportive tasks for hands, not challenging tasks for minds. Central Office approbation was reserved for the traditional backroom role. We were back to the situation when I had taken over, when agents and constituency chairmen alike told me: 'The women love stuffing envelopes, it gives them something to do.'

*

I left Conservative Central Office under a cloud after a row with Norman Tebbit over my wooing of Asian and black women for the Conservative Party. On the back of my 'high-flyers' conference cycle I had organized a first Asian women's conference and planned another one, together with a conference for black professional women. These initiatives proved highly popular with the Asian professionals who came and spoke; they were impressed with the listening ear offered to them. We were set fair for success with the limited task I had set the women's organization of opening up our work to these exceptional achievers and asking them if they were willing to get involved in party politics. However, this was too revolutionary for the traditional Central Office approach to drumming up party support.

I was dismayed and saddened by the Party Chairman's attitude, but it became clear to me that my days at Central Office were numbered. My marching orders came immediately after the 1987 general election, albeit with the nicest of letters from Mrs Thatcher. It seemed to me that she felt rather shamefaced at her shabby treatment of someone who had given unstintingly as a volunteer to the cause of the Conservative women's organization.

Chapter 6

West Devon and Westminster

My first constituency was Blyth, a mining seat; my second was Devon West and Torridge, where the local wealth came from farming and Dartmoor, tourists and clotted cream. Between the two lay a period of heavy interviewing for different seats. Following the 1983 election and Willie Whitelaw's elevation to the House of Lords, I nearly fought the Penrith and the Borders by-election. I came second to David Maclean, whose agent subsequently left the Conservatives to head Sir James Goldsmith's Referendum Party in 1996. Later on I was interviewed for Torbay; Conservative Torbay and I formed a mutual and instant dislike. I also went for Surbiton, where a close friend, Nigel Fisher, was retiring, and other safe-ish Tory seats. I started to come second, but realized that my liberal views sat most uneasily with almost every selection committee – much more so than in my earlier selection round in 1975. I also sensed a worrying dislocation between those selecting candidates and the realities of modern life. I found I needed to put myself back in time significantly in order to strike the chords the various committee members wanted to hear.

Why was it that I suited and Devon West and Torridge and they suited me? This was a vast constituency of nearly a thousand square miles, home to almost four thousand farmers and encompassing both the beauties of Dartmoor and its bleak prison at the far end near the old stannary (tin-mining) town of Tavistock. In the villages a newer stratum of incomers was gradually emerging, people who, on retirement, wished to return to some earlier holiday experience, recalling the quietness, the scenery or the seaside hospitality they had first enjoyed, perhaps, as children. They tended to play an active part in village committees – which was fine until, having filled all the committee positions for which the farmers had less and less time, they took the local decisions which superimposed urban values on countrymen and women whose families had tilled the earth and run the marketplaces for perhaps eight generations. A constituent once complained to me that the green view from his window had been replaced by a yellow one. I was to change it back again, fast. In fact, I telephoned the farmer and congratulated him on his new profit centre of oil-seed rape. He laughed with satisfaction. I guess my suitability for the people of Torridge and West Devon lay in my liberal roots, which, as for the farmers, grew out of centuries of countryside traditions.

In terms of political history it was a very interesting constituency. The first recorded MP for Okehampton was Sir Robertus Cissor in 1300. In addition to the great eighteenth-century statesman William Pitt, Thomas Pitt and Robert Pitt also sat for the small town of Okehampton. In one heady moment the town elected four MPs, when even by prevailing standards of rotten boroughs two should have sufficed. Members of Parliament for this constituency had also been high on individualism and low on conformity. One controversial Member was Edward Thomas, a member of the Long Parliament who in 1648 was barred from the House of Commons for disagreeing with the King; and six or seven had crossed the floor or resigned the whip in living memory.

I was astonished when the sitting MP, Peter Mills, tendered his resignation. It turned out he had cancer and, nearing sixty-five, felt it best not to stand again. A prominent member of the Conservative Women's National Committee told me not to put my name forward: the constituency did not want a woman and was not going to interview any. She added that this message had gone round all women candidates. Women should not apply. I thought for a moment or two. I knew the constituency must be out of my reach but I felt I should give it a try. As a country person, brought up on a farm, I believed I would understand the farmers' problems and be able to articulate them strongly. In any case, interviews were good practice. One of these days, I thought, I might actually win. So I put my name down.

Against the odds I was selected from nearly 270 people who applied for the long-list of thirty-seven to be interviewed. At that time it was a safe Conservative seat and I was clear in my own mind I was not going to win: I went down for practice. The interview was in a country inn, in Hatherleigh village. Ducking the fourteenth-century beams, I thoroughly enjoyed myself, knowing I would not be back. I learned afterwards that I had got the interview because the elderly agent had told the selection committee that they might seem rather old-fashioned as an association if they interviewed no women at all. Since I had applied, he argued, and since as Party Vice-Chairman I must be respectable, why not see me just once? After all, I need go no further in the process. The interview was fun; I liked the farmers, and I then enjoyed the rest of the weekend fact-finding elsewhere in the constituency.

To my delight and astonishment I was called for a second interview. Again, I knew I should treat it just as practice. This time there was a larger audience, asking many of the same questions. I arrived, enjoyed myself again and left.

A month later I was called back again. I nearly took fright. This was for real. I did my worst speech by far and stumbled over the constituency name, calling it 'Torrington', not 'Torridge', but recovered my footing in questions. I was asked what I thought about badgers. I replied that the link with bovine tuberculosis was not proven; nevertheless I thought the jury was still out, and that where herds were infected, badgers should be eradicated. I gathered later that other candidates talked warmly about badgers as nice furry creatures to an audience composed of farmers suffering bad losses from dairy herds infected with TB.

This third round took place in Hatherleigh Town Hall, where I held my wedding reception two years later. Four of us were still in the running, and as we waited for our turn we were kept fuelled with cups of tea at the back by Marjorie Cleverdon, the wife of the selection committee chairman. Marjorie was a local organist and a lovely person. To my astonishment I was chosen to go forward for ratification by the General Council. As the hall broke up in comfortable confusion, I overheard a local cub reporter from the *Western Morning News*, the regional daily, asking an elderly farmer (who, I subsequently found out, was a member of the notorious Monday Club) why I had been chosen. 'Surely,' the reporter said, 'you were going to choose a local man, preferably a farmer.'

'Yes,' said the farmer.

'So why haven't you?' asked the reporter. 'You have chosen a woman from outside.'

'Well, you know how it is,' replied the other, 'when you chooses a prize cow. You looks at her feet and you looks at her walk and you looks at her pedigree and then you buys her. Us has done all that and we've bought her.'

I could not help but laugh. But I knew what he meant. Members of Parliament are there to serve their constituencies.

I felt at home immediately. I left the Save the Children Fund, moved into a small house on Hatherleigh High Street and worked to understand the needs of those who would, I hoped, become my own constituents. I offered a personal commitment more than a political ideology. I dedicated myself to work for their good, and to use my background in industrial and social welfare to find ways and means of helping the people to help themselves effectively. My closest friend among the Conservatives was Margaret Fry. As well as chairing the CWNC she was a farmer's daughter, a farmer's wife, a Young Farmers' Union member and an enthusiast for any cause she fought.

I felt wholly comfortable with the farmers. Although their tenure only stretched back eight generations at the most – to the time when the coming of the railways made possible the transport of milk and sheep and so enabled profitable farming as opposed to merely subsistence cultivation – their families formed the heart of the social structure in each village and market town. I believed strongly that my core task was to protect and enhance their way of life. It really didn't matter to me which way they voted, provided a sufficient number kept me in a position which would allow me to help them flourish.

The two years between selection and election were tough and furious with activity. My bank manager told me I could not get into Parliament on an overdraft from him. So I took up part-time work in the Duke of Edinburgh's Award Scheme, working for Prince Philip and Prince Edward, to whom I was deputy chairman, setting up committees of young people under Prince Edward's chairmanship. Subsequently, the Duke of Edinburgh asked me to become Chairman of the Friends of the Duke of Edinburgh's Award Scheme; sadly, by that stage my parliamentary work curtailed this involvement. I also worked for Westminster Children's Hospital, trying to keep it open – though Peter Brooke, in whose constituency the hospital was, did not support its retention, and without his backing no political ground could be gained – and for the World Association of Girl Guides and Girl Scouts, a cheerful, hardworking and far-flung organization, and as a consultant for another large children's charity. Together, these interests brought in just enough money to keep myself afloat.

Most of my time was spent in Devon, getting to know the personalities in the Conservative association and its various branches. At this time there were eighty-three branches, nearly all active, constantly carrying out fund-raising events. I raced from one to another, covering three in an average Saturday evening, returning at the end of my travels to my small cottage. Here I was surrounded by Labour voters, thin on the ground in that part of Devon. The Methodist church was at the bottom of the street, and I went there as regularly as to the Anglican parish church. In both the music was superlative, and the vicar and minister were such good friends that combined services took place regularly. I was, however, rebuked by the local Conservative chairman when I attended midnight service at Christmas in the Methodist church. This was not right, he said: the Conservatives worshipped in the parish church, and I must be there with them. I disliked these divisions, which in this part of the country reflected social divisions. I continued to be a member of both, and a year later married Michael in the Methodist church. George Thomas, now Lord Tonypandy, read the lesson. Within twenty-four hours, after a crowded service and reception, I received a message from my agent at the hotel in Somerset where we were on our honeymoon. 'The election is on,' it said. 'Come back at once.'

A month later, the election won, I gave a speech to my new constituents. I pledged myself to serve the constituency and in particular to work to free up market forces, starting the slow claw-back of nationalized institutions into private ownership. I firmly claimed that the Conservative goal was national unity and that the crucial task was to heal the divisions between north and south, rich and poor, immigrant and native, unionized and non-unionized, worker and unemployed. I added that we must use our power sensitively, balance realism with understanding and implement hard economic decisions with compassion. Everything I touched on was going to be difficult to achieve, but what in life that was worth doing could be easy?

I entered the House of Commons in June 1987, walking along the same passages and into the same rooms as many of my political ancestors had done before me. Much of the Palace of Westminster had been rebuilt by Barry and Pugin in the middle of the nineteenth century following the great fire of 1834; only my great-grandfathers or succeeding generations would have known those parts. But the Cloisters, where I was given a desk, were medieval; and the beauty of the eleventh-century Great Hall, with its thirteenth-century high vaulting and hammer-beam roof, would have been familiar to my earliest political forebears.

More than the architecture had changed in recent years. Why do so many Members seek to put their questions to the minister on duty after the magic hour of 3.00 p.m., rather than half an hour earlier when questions start? They are striving to catch the Speaker's eye within the window of live television coverage. There was strong opposition to the introduction of television into the House of Commons on the grounds that the intrusion would disrupt debate. This it certainly did. It was extraordinary to see, from the moment the cameras first appeared, how MPs would attempt to play to them. There is a little red light on top of each of the five cameras within the chamber which glows to show that it is in operation. The red lights had to be removed so Members would not be able to tell which camera to play to; but still they tried, turning to face one camera after another. And yet the opponents of televising the House of Commons – Margaret Thatcher, of course, among them – seemed to me to overlook the way in which the public now gathered their news. If we wanted Parliament to be accessible we had to use up-to-date methods of communication. While acknowledging the force of some of the arguments against, therefore, I spoke, and voted, in favour. For me, the House was a servant of the people; our work should be transparent.

Ensuring that its work was transparent to me as a participant depended in part on making sure I could hear what was going on. Reaction to my pronounced hearing loss varies. The Conservative Women's National Committee had always dealt with it in a practical, uncontroversial and unobtrusive way. They behaved quite properly as if there were no problem unless I asked for repetition or clarification of a point that I had missed. Elsewhere in my career I'd had an even simpler time: nobody noticed. In the House of Commons it was very different. For one thing, the media pounced on it straight away. Far and away the most thoughtful person in my new environment was Robin Maxwell Hyslop, the long-serving Conservative Member for Tiverton. Robin was a most engaging political personality. In his chosen field of parliamentary procedure he had no equal on the benches on either side during the time I was with him in the House of Commons. He would leap up, fiercely indignant, at some perceived and apparently trivial procedural oversight quite unremarked by anyone other than himself. People wondered why he bothered. But in parliamentary politics – as in so many organizations up to and including the United Nations – argument over the rules and their interpretation holds a dominant position in the business of each day, because time is the one weapon that parliamentarians outside the golden circle of the Executive have at their disposal, leaving aside the ultimate weapon, the 'nuclear option' of voting against your own side. It is those who control the timetabling of Parliamentary business, the order of play, the length of speeches, who usually control the outcome of debates.

Robin chaired the Devon group of MPs (all the county's Members in 1987 were Conservative, save one in Plymouth). He made absolutely sure that I understood every word that was said. Without a request from me – the ultimate in kindness – he kept his chairman's eye keenly alert and slipped me a note from time to time when he saw that I had missed a point. It made an unbelievable difference. Robin, and so many of the other Tory Members who left in 1992, epitomized the public service ethos of those who would never have entered politics for personal gain. They are very sorely missed.

Within the Chamber, as I had anticipated, I was able to make use of the amplifiers embedded in the backs of the benches. This was not without its own hazards. I suffered consistent headaches sitting among the Conservatives, because the sheer racket, the actual noise level they created yelling at the Opposition every day, pushed the decibel count beyond my pain threshold. Labour Members, on the whole, were very thoughtful; but I noted that the Liberals, and later the Liberal Democrats, were consistently the most civilized. Some Conservatives were continually obstructive. I'd never felt handicapped before.

I initiated debates in an attempt to bring in legislation to maximize the availability of critically needed hearing aids throughout the United Kingdom. This was a touchy topic. The NHS clutched the provision of these useful and skilfully engineered devices to its heart, claiming that the correction of hearing was such a sensitive matter that only the NHS could be trusted to do it properly. Whenever I raised the matter, hurt or even angry NHS professionals would write in claiming that the private providers of hearing aids were ruffians, charlatans or even worse. The problem was, the NHS just could not cope with even diagnosing the millions of people in the United Kingdom who needed hearing aids. The provision of technical equipment is essential for a condition which medicine can barely touch. If you have a hearing defect which can be corrected by surgical intervention you are very unusual. NHS hearing aids often do not fit, do not match the hearing loss and are therefore cast aside by their users, who are thus left without any assistance at all. One of the greatest follies of the existing system that I could see was that the NHS, in its most suffocating of maternal modes, insisted on providing batteries by post for everyone to whom an NHS aid was prescribed. The cost must be unbelievable – all for tiny batteries, the size of a little fingernail, which can be bought at a corner shop for very little. It would be better to issue a small grant with each hearing aid to fund the battery supply. Talk about a culture of dependency! Yet I could not get successive health ministers to treat the matter with proper seriousness.

Outside the Commons, I was a trouble to many of the deaf membership associations. I did not fit their pattern. I gave a talk to the children at Britain's only grammar school for the deaf, which was near to my family home – indeed, my mother had been a governor there. I talked to the children about how to get ahead as deaf people in a hearing world. The children loved it, but some of the parents said that I must be a fraud. No one could talk as I did or handle the work that I had done with a severe hearing loss. I gave up trying to help the deaf community, regretfully, but believing that Jack Ashley MP, brave and succeeding after a catastrophic mid-life hearing loss, was a better champion for them and a fine example for them to follow.

For many Conservative Members of Parliament, my disability – any disability – was an embarrassment. It was not a topic they wanted to discuss. Peter Thurnham had to struggle to set up his Conservative Disability Group against the cold prevailing tide of Conservative opinion. Nick Scott, as minister for the disabled, moved mountains. In any other party he would have achieved heroic stature, but among the Tories his work was merely tolerated and he was just 'good old Nick'. And it was difficult to admire Lady Olga Maitland when, at the Whips' command, she infamously spent a Friday morning blocking Opposition amendments to the Government Disability Bill, misleading the House in the process and heaping shame upon an already shameful episode.

The structure of the Conservative Party in Central Office and the country was very familiar to me: I had been at more branch meetings than I could count as a child with my father, and as Party Vice-Chairman I had got to grips with both the voluntary and salaried structure in Conservative Central Office and the area and local associations in the country. But the structure of the parliamentary party was new to me and somehow different from the picture my father had painted. The 1922 Committee of backbench MPs still existed and technically ran the shop. It met every Thursday at six o'clock, in the largest Committee Room, Number Fourteen, in Committee Room Corridor. The room was always packed. All the Members of the Commons tried to come, as did many Members of the

Lords. This was the forum where the backbenchers were meant to be free to speak up, to criticize their leaders if they wished, away from the Government and free from fear of disciplinary reaction. Free from surveillance, however, they definitely were not. The boundaries had blurred, of course, with the creation of the post of PPS: the Parliamentary Private Secretaries, the ministers' alter egos, were still technically backbenchers, so they were there – by the time I left, some fifty-eight of them – and the Whips were represented too.

The meetings were very short. Five minutes was the norm, and six minutes was thought to be too long. The Executive Committee, a prefect-like body, sat at the top. The chairman opened the meeting, called for the minutes (all of two sentences) and agreed them; then he maybe made a declaration himself if something had to be announced, and asked the Whip on duty to read out the next week's business. Members would take out their pens and scribble down the whipping for seven days from the following Monday. Occasionally a brave soul would object to a particularly heavy whip, perhaps late on a Thursday night, which meant he could not get back to the south-west or Scotland. The complaint was always deflected and the complainant told to talk to the Whip on duty. A grudging call for any other business – not encouraged – and that was it.

This was no check on the Executive at all. And the barking of curt orders from the Chairman to the Whip on duty, and from the Whip to the Members, contradicted the sole purpose of the 1922 Committee, which was to be a voice of influence from the Members on the Government.

Doubtless this formula had been adhered to for some years. A more recent and equally regrettable feature was the complete loss of confidentiality. When any interesting business was afoot, the media, the lobby correspondents, would stand outside Committee Room Fourteen and, as members surged out, grab likely people or perhaps those they had under agreement to spill the beans. Some three hours later the same evening, the *Nine o'Clock News* would feature an exact report, verbatim in some cases, of what had been said.

Even the new select committee system, set up in the early eighties to offer an alternative method of scrutinizing an overwhelmingly powerful Executive, was becoming increasingly hamstrung as time passed. These committees could only fulfil the purpose for which they were designed if they were not whipped. So no official places on them had been set aside for Whips. Gradually, however, their independence was eroded by an informal whipping system. I experienced its pressure in the Select Committee on Employment in the early 1990s, when it was made very plain to all of us on the Conservative side that we must vote on party lines and support party policy. A whole new system to monitor the Executive had been set up at vast expense, not least in travel costs, and in the end the only truly independent mind remaining was in many cases that of the Committee Clerk, who generally wrote the reports in any case.

The impoverishment of parliamentary business went further. Like other Members of Parliament I sat on single-party groups, backbench committees on particular areas of policy interest. Once, these had been the focus of intensive discussions and debates, with members afterwards going in to the Smoking Room for a drink together. Now they were tiny in number and threadbare in membership; Conservative Members attended them only rarely, perhaps because of the increased weight of postbags and the growth of offices, staffed by secretaries, within the parliamentary buildings. One permanent feature was, of course, the subject Whip, who wrote down Members' comments and reported back to his masters, reprimanding and marking the files of anyone who, like myself, strayed from the Government line. Such surveillance, moreover, was not restricted to the various groups in which a Member might participate; conversations overheard in the tea room could call forth similar reproof for remarks less than slavishly loyal.

All-party groups, on the other hand, I found to be far more

to my style, well attended and project-orientated. I started a number myself and accepted election to others. This gave me a welcome opportunity to get together with people of different backgrounds to look seriously at particular problems we faced at home or to make links with other Parliaments abroad.

The standing committees were different again. These existed to scrutinize detailed legislation fresh from the floor of the House. And there was lots of it. Indeed, my deepest initial concern with Mrs Thatcher's leadership was the weight of legislation that she triggered. It became a proof of virility for her ministers to have a Bill in a Queen's Speech. This proliferation of measures meant that the impact of each proposed addition to the Statute Book on legislation already in existence, or indeed on the life of the ordinary citizen, could not be fully thought through. The pressure to produce proposals also meant that legislation came to the House ill-prepared and imperfectly digested even by the sponsoring department. Each Bill trailed shelves of amending documents in its wake. The confusion resulting from the welter of additional, often complex, legislative minutiae could do untold damage. The poll tax debacle was only the worst example.

Struggling through one piece of legislation after another as ministers turned up with a printed Bill in one hand and already a clutch of amendments in the other, the standing committees could not apply the microscopic scrutiny for which they were designed. Inevitably, the attention they could pay to the material was patchy and often based on false assumptions. This flood of documentation was matched by the snowdrift of regulations, which intensified my concern about Government bypassing any parliamentary scrutiny of profound changes to so many aspects of citizens' lives. My concern was further amplified by the malign, even warped, intentions that seemed to me to be embodied in some of these changes.

The Standing Committee on Statutory Instruments, some of which dealt with topics of considerable importance to the electorate, came increasingly to be treated with derision by the

Whips. Members who wished to speak, other than the front-bench spokesmen, were often crudely dealt with. In May 1995 I heard a Member object to the Whip, saying angrily that, since he was not allowed to speak at all and the subject was one on which he had much information, the committee was a farce. I tended to agree with him. I faced the same problem in June 1995 with the Draft Arts Council (Northern Ireland) Order. Two years earlier I had set up a Northern Ireland ADAPT, separate from the original Scottish-based body but similarly dedicated to achieving access for disabled people to arts premises and public libraries. This Order was of importance to the organization, as was well known to the Northern Ireland Office. I tried to raise the Order before the committee; the Whip tried to stop me. I insisted on speaking for all of two minutes, earning myself a subsequent rebuke. At least that statutory instrument went in front of the committee, however cursorily. Most of the hailstorm of regulations that the Government was raising saw no committee at all: thus MPs had no opportunity to comment on this fungoid growth of secondary legislation. Ministers could act unchecked.

Issues of social importance came to the fore with work for my constituency in Parliament. For some time I had been a member of the Howard League for Penal Reform. An interest in penal policy was natural for me, given my constituency responsibility. I met Dartmoor prisoners in surgeries I held inside the gaol, at first by courtesy of Governor John May, who subsequently rose to be the Regional Director of HM Prisons, despite an unprecedented three votes of no confidence in him by Dartmoor's Prison Officers' Association, in reaction against his rehabilitative policies. In fact, the Princetown POA was a good group of men, who even allowed the odd woman in as Deputy Governor from time to time.

But Dartmoor was a prison that should have been resited somewhere near Plymouth or even Cardiff, or one of the other major cities of Wales or the south-west. Its remote and inaccessible location on the moor was in direct opposition to the modern view, borne out by studies of prisoners and former prisoners, that building up inmates' fragile personal relationships with friends and families might be the key component in preventing recidivism. As it was, prisoners' families had to struggle for hours, sometimes days and nights, to get to Princetown village, where they were put up by the Wesley Centre, of which I became the Patron. This was run by a voluntary group, led by Methodists but open to people of any denomination or none, set up to help strengthen prisoners' family relationships in the hope of giving them a sounder base on which to build a life away from crime after their release.

But Dartmoor was not handed over to the National Trust to become a bleak but wonderful hotel; nor was it left to decay as a foreboding ruin in deference to Sherlock Holmes. Instead, Conservative Governments poured millions and millions of pounds into building work to shore up this oldest of Britain's penal institutions. Built by French prisoners in the Napoleonic Wars to entomb them until they died, the prison remains, despite extensive and continuing modernization, a place where the nineteenth-century belief in isolation as the best medicine for the offender's soul remains unchallenged.

Devon is fierce in its sentencing policy. The county's magistrates seem to pass more custodial sentences than those of other counties, despite the fact that the effectiveness of prison sentences is limited to keeping the sentenced outside civil society for as long as they are confined. For a certain period of time their violence, in whatever form of crime it was expressed, is bottled up; but it is neither treated nor eradicated, and so they come out and reoffend. Rehabilitation is the only way to break this depressing and futile cycle. But constructive care is, it seems, in short supply even for those who should not be in prison in the first place: the hospital wings of prison after prison are now filled with those who formerly would have been in medical care outside the prison walls but have been either ill served or wholly abandoned by society through the dramatic underfunding of the 'Care in the Community' programme.

The agenda for prison reform since 1987 has been set by the Woolf Report (co-authored by Judge Stephen Tumim). Liberal in thrust, it focused on prisoner rehabilitation. However, moves in this direction have been blocked by Michael Howard, who as Home Secretary appears to have been driven in his penal policy by the desire to gain support for the Government from *Daily Mail* readers. Prison governors have been remorselessly squeezed by the pressures put on them by a Home Secretary who has presided over both constraints on the prison budget and a sharp rise in the prison population. They cannot cut accommodation, food or prison officers; therefore they take the only remaining option, cutting probation services, education, training and work programmes – in short, cutting humanity out of the system.

Dartmoor Prison had recently been downgraded and now took few Category A prisoners, the real hard cases who had been in and out for most of their lives. I had stopped asking what they were in for, as the lists of sentence details were so voluminous. The prisoners now were Category Bs and Cs: younger men, maybe on their third or fourth stretch and with perhaps just four years to serve. Just the kind of prisoners, one might think, who could most effectively, and most productively, be targeted for rehabilitative treatment.

I had some notable successes from time to time. I took up the case of one man due to be deported to India in a matter of weeks. His crime, for which he had served five years, was drug running: he had been caught at Heathrow, coming in from New York, with sufficient drugs on him for Customs and Excise to prove guilt to the court's satisfaction. The court saw that he had been born in India and sentenced him to deportation there after his prison sentence had been served. He wanted to meet me, and the prison officers passed on his request. I was wandering around the prison at the time chatting to the prisoners in what is called free association time, namely the short period after the last meal of the day, early in the evening, in which prisoners are allowed to mix and mingle before being locked in their cells for the night. This could be one case out of thousands, they felt, which might have some merit. Perhaps there was nothing in it, they said, but they just had an instinct. It might be worth my taking a look.

The prisoner came forward and we had a talk. I was given his file; the heavy folder was full of pleadings from his solicitor, each one turned down, in which the claim was made that he was not Indian and had no friends or family in the country, so should not be deported; and, moreover, that he was not guilty, at least not of the crime for which he had been convicted. I heard such stories regularly. But I decided to take this one up.

I was lucky in that at this period the Home Secretary kept changing, which allowed me to keep asking as if each request were the first. The weeks and months passed and the deportation was not carried out; and eventually I won a re-examination of the case. By this time the prisoner's mother was sick with shingles through worry and his father was in hospital after a severe heart attack. The question of Indian nationality, it turned out, had arisen because the father had served in the Indian air force; his son, therefore, was born in that country. But they had no Indian-based relations and their lives were as British as could be. One daughter was married to a senior officer at the Australian Embassy in London; another was working in the City. Not only did the Home Office admit that deportation to India would be a real miscarriage of justice but, against the longest of odds, we'd broken through the sentence. The Home Secretary informed me by letter that the prisoner had been wrongly accused on trumped-up evidence and that those who created it had now admitted this. Eureka! We had won. I could not believe it. It was an incredible triumph. The man repaired his marriage; he brought his children, both under ten, to see me. He got a job. He entered the Open University.

From time to time thereafter he dropped into Central Lobby to tell me all was well.

Such cases were very rare indeed. But as prisoners who knew of me in Dartmoor moved around Britain after they had left, their friends got to hear of the work I had done for someone, and soon small streams of letters were coming in from all over the UK. It was natural, therefore, that I should accept invitations to join the Board of the Howard League for Penal Reform and the Penal Affairs Group. It remains the case that any prisoner can write to any Member of Parliament from anywhere in the United Kingdom and still get a hearing, if the MP is willing.

Chapter 7

An Uphill Struggle

Among the most pressing problems of my Devon constituency were those of schoolchildren and teachers. To start with, school buildings were in a terrible state. Even before I became an MP I had begun work on this difficult issue in the case of Dolton Primary School, two villages away from my own. I could hardly believe what I was hearing from the teachers on the telephone, but when I went to see for myself, everything they said was true. The children had outdoor lavatories, some of which did not even have roofs: they looked like cow byres, primitive cob structures made of mud and straw, open to the sky. Prolonged battering at the ministry door and a friendly minister, Bob Dunn, accompanied by the local bishop (it was a church-aided school) produced an ingenious answer. Unspent funds for the forthcoming financial year, as yet unidentified, would be pre-allocated. Thirty thousand pounds emerged and Dolton Primary School received its building.

That was a satisfying result; but Dolton was only the tip of the iceberg. At the other end of the constituency, I discovered, Horrabridge County Primary school was in an astonishing condition. No child in Horrabridge was taught in a permanent building which could be called a school. Instead, all of their lessons took place a half hour's walk away from the original school building, now used for offices, and over three major roads, in temporary huts which had been put up twenty or thirty years previously and now oozed damp through cardboard walls. Tavistock County Primary school was also in trouble. The building was an old one, delightful for lovers of Victorian architecture but impossible for modern teachers; and it was packed. This was an enormously successful school in terms of pupil happiness and progress. The head teacher, Antony Wate, had lived in south-east Asia for a time in his youth; when he came back he worked in a shipping company in Liverpool before going back into education. He was now determined to make sure that none of 'his' children lost their opportunities. I played at a concert there to help them raise funds and joined their pressure group for change. Okehampton County Primary, where the town mayor, Joan Pauley, had taught for a long time, much of it as head, was another venerable structure where the classrooms were inadequate for modern children's needs.

Devon's population was growing too fast and the children just could not fit in. Even a staunch Conservative councillor like Mary Vick knew that it had been years of inactivity and lack of interest on the part of the Conservative County Council that had led to so many dilapidated schools in my constituency. These decaying buildings posed a significant risk to children's health. Holsworthy Community College was an even worse example. Head teacher Malcolm Woodward showed me the physical damage. Here again, second- or third-hand prefabricated buildings, trucked in and settled on concrete sites as a temporary expedient, had remained in use for decades. The walls were wet inside. No wonder that even in the soft air of rural Devon the children's chests suffered and asthma was on the increase. In July 1996 the Thornbury Parish Clerk, Mr R. Birkett, wrote to me on the plight of Bradford County Primary School: 'They currently have around 70 pupils on the register and only TWO CLASSROOMS. This clearly causes them great difficulty in physically containing the children and also in delivering the requirements of the National Curriculum.'

Time after time I went to the minister in London; occasionally, in response to my badgering, small amounts of funding were disgorged. But Government ministers seemed obdurate in their refusal to change the overall policy to tackle the underlying problem. Educational building has, it seems to me, been reduced to the status of a political plaything.

Teacher numbers were another continuing problem. Gillian Shephard herself, when Secretary of State for Education, assured me that there would be no teacher cuts in 1995, despite the cut in the education budget. She suggested that the warning of imminent staff reductions was a party political ploy by the Liberal Democrats and that no teachers would lose their jobs. In fact, hundreds of teachers' jobs were lost in Devon alone: 144 redundancies were made in the single year 1995/6, and even this figure does not include the losses that arise from the non-renewal of short-term contracts. When these occurred she claimed they didn't count because classroom assistant numbers were growing.

For the Secretary of State thus to claim that classroom assistants could carry out the jobs of teachers was too far down the line of misunderstanding for me to tolerate. Extra teachers were urgently needed *as well as* classroom assistants. Implementation of the recommendations of the excellent Warnock Report of 1981 had put into action the philosophy that children of all abilities and patterns of behaviour should be educated in the mainstream schools. This had resulted in an influx of children with 'special needs', often manifested in severe learning difficulties, which made much greater demands on teaching and pastoral staff. Children with IQs of 80 and 160 were being educated in the same streams in the same schools. There was a critical need for classroom assistants to enable the under-achievers to fulfil their potential, and also to help maintain order in classes including children with acute behavioural problems, generally derived from disastrous relationships within their families. Lack of support from home triggered disruptive behaviour in class and stopped children learning. Violence in the classroom was an increasing problem, and school playgrounds in many villages had become the target of adult drug dealers. Teachers and classroom assistants alike did a magnificent job despite suffering from consistent and often severe stress. As I got closer to those who worked in the schools I realized that crowd control was a better description of the role that had been forced upon them by successive Conservative Governments.

As the children grew up I saw them try for college. Opening the gates of higher education to vastly increased numbers of entrants was a wonderful concept, but it would only work without a drop in standards if student numbers and expenditure on the institutions to which they flocked increased in parallel; and Britain's economy couldn't easily afford the same quality of higher education for such a high proportion of school-leavers. The stress on the system was exacerbated by the introduction into the academic world of management consultancy techniques and commercial accountability, resulting in a hugely increased load of paperwork for tutors. The higher education system as a whole began to suffer. Tutorials became too large to merit the name; teachers started either to miss or to lose interest in their lectures. The assumption was made that all higher education was the same. This both undervalued the excellence of the academic elite and downgraded the value of degrees across the board. Exams were marked by relatively lower standards. Able young people felt desperate through lack of personal challenge. As in so many other areas of policy, the Conservative Government talked about quality but concentrated on quantity. And while this was taking place, educational policy in other EU nations, geared towards competitiveness, was enabling their young people to reach ever greater academic heights.

Health care was another problem for West Devon. People became anxious as the excellent small hospitals which formed the backbone of local health provision came under threat of closure. I approached a Government minister who said there was nothing that could be done. The Department of Health was not minded to try to keep these hospitals open; in fact, they were being shut everywhere. I fought back and prevented the hospitals being closed; but Government hostility to their continued existence was fierce and continuous.

Another institution of immense importance in rural life which came under threat from the Conservative Government was the sub-post office, the nub of many communities. Ninety-two sub-post offices flourished in my constituency in 1987. These were a lifeline for pensioners and mothers especially. After all, most villages had only one bus service a week to take them to the nearest market town; how else could they get their pensions and child benefit? Few working families had more than one car. Only 50 per cent of the British people had bank accounts and most of the pensioners and young mothers in my constituency were not among them. Child benefit was critically important to families in areas where jobs were in short supply. The extra pounds a week each child attracted could make the difference between keeping the family farm going and selling up. In the privacy of their kitchens farmers often showed me their account books, compiled at the end of each year by their wives. Sometimes the net annual income was under two thousand pounds – without allowing any pay for the wife's work, day in and day out, as both housewife and farm helper. Without child benefit the position would have been untenable; and without the village post office, how would she get it? Little by little, despite all efforts, the sub-post offices started to close. Some ingenious negotiation with Post Office Chairman Sir Bryan Nicholson's office brought him to the constituency three times, where he gained a crucial understanding of the vital necessity of the sub-post office system. He and his staff found ways and means of assisting the sub-postmasters and mistresses to keep going. But again the Government did not grasp the general point, the indispensability to the community of the existing system. More sub-post offices closed. Gradually the spectre of privatization began to loom.

The farms in West Devon were not very large compared with those of the Home Counties and East Anglia. Productivity was generally lower, too, held down by the poorer quality of much of the land, which was mostly Grades 3 and 4, the two bottom agricultural classifications. The problem was rainfall: only the Lake District had a higher rainfall per annum than Dartmoor. It made for wonderful green grass, and luxurious cloudscapes to attract amateur artists, of whom there were plenty; but it made the production of high-quality, highly profitable grain impossible. The answer was grazing, and my constituency contained thousands of sheep and cattle which grazed their way to a generally meagre income for the farmers.

Few of the farmers down here would have survived without the Common Agricultural Policy. The milk quota brought in a windfall capital gain to dairy farmers. However, it created a problem for the country as a whole as it meant Britain producing 80 per cent of the dairy products consumed by the population and importing the rest. This meant that the local cheese and butter factories in Torrington and North Tawton were under continual threat. Dairycrest in Torrington succumbed; while Eden Vale in North Tawton operated permanently at half its capacity and was eventually sold on to an Irish company.

The sheep producers fought for quota too, particularly in view of the fluctuating levels of the Hill Farmers' Livestock Compensatory Allowance. This small annual injection of cash from the European Union enabled upland farmers to survive on the sparse grassland and under harsh weather conditions. The meat that was produced from the hillsides, from Dartmoor at any rate, was fine and sweet. In the early 1990s the Dartmoor farmers created a niche market by shipping live lambs to France where, once killed, they could be labelled 'French lamb'. Weighing about twelve kilos, as opposed to the ordinary sixteen to twenty kilos, they gave the right size of joints for the fastidious Parisian housewives' cooking pots. That trade, however, fell foul of the RSPCA campaign in the mid-1990s for a ban on the export of live animals to other EU countries, fuelled by under-cover film showing the atrocious conditions in which animals were transported and killed, particularly in Spain.

The greatest agricultural crisis of recent years, of course, has been that associated with the problem of BSE. Many farmers' livelihoods might have been saved, and a great deal of anxiety in many quarters avoided, had the Government acted sooner and in a more thoughtful fashion. Beef and dairy farmers were troubled about the ingredients in cattle feed before I entered Parliament. They wanted legislation forcing the feed companies to list ingredients. As a member, I put down questions in 1988 and 1989 calling for compulsory labelling. The Government refused to act. Later, in 1996, minister Tony Baldry attacked cattle farmers on television for feeding animals with potentially BSE-infected feedstuff, having declined to give them the information that would have enabled them to avoid doing so.

Moreover, since the Government did not take BSE seriously, paying only half the market value for a BSE-infected animal and allowing the herd to stay alive and ultimately be consumed by humans, some farmers were less than scrupulous in response. The extinction of much of the knackers' industry did not help. Carcasses were disposed of more cheaply in ways which paid less regard to human health than formerly. Water supplies were particularly vulnerable to illicit burials. Staff at the Ministry of Agriculture were culled themselves, and the vital middle management level, crucial in carrying out monitoring of regula-tions and practices, disappeared. ADAS, the advisory profes-sionals, were pushed towards privatization and began to charge for their services. BSE struck down thousands of cattle. Export controls were tightened drastically, but the British consumer was still allowed to purchase meat deemed potentially infected by the EU and already unacceptable (on grounds of treatment by hormones) in the United States and Brazil as early as 1988.

In 1994 farmers told me how they were evading the EU export restraints. Why should they not? they said. If their beef was good enough for Britain, why not for the continent too? It was a clever fiddle, but a dangerous one: potentially infected cattle continued to get through to France, Italy, Germany and beyond. The agriculture minister Gillian Shephard did not take it seriously. I concluded that MAFF ministers were irresponsible in their approach to public health. A new post of public health minister should be created, and kept strictly separate from any commercial interest.

*

In 1987, only 11 per cent of the new MPs had previously worked in business or industry. The number of Conservative Members who have experience of the world of work outside politics is now very small indeed, and shrinking fast. The constriction of view this represents was demonstrated vividly when I discovered Conservative MPs laughing at the concept of equal pay for work of equal value. I realized that they had neither experienced the need for it, nor felt any urge to implement it. The progressive loss of knowledge and experience from the House of Commons on the Conservative side has drastic implications for the conduct of its business. Members are legislating on things they know nothing about. This became particularly obvious to me in the course of work on the 1988 Copyright Act, during which I put forward over a period of eight months a round of amendments – which were accepted in the end – to protect computer software copyright. I was told I had made more changes to Government legislation than any backbencher had ever done before. This was innovative legislation, and it was tough going explaining to colleagues what I meant. They had no experience: to them, computers were something their eleven-year-old sons played with. Yet information technology is one of Europe's biggest export industries, second only to tourism.

The Standing Committee on the Copyright Bill, on which I sat, was made up of a most interesting group of people. Tony Blair led for the Opposition and John Butcher for the Government. Alan Howarth was the Government Whip. He said: 'My job is to get the government's legislation through.' I said: 'My task is to get the right legislation through for copyright protection.' While I was struggling to get through a particularly critical amendment, the minister, John Butcher, kept saying: 'No! No! No!' I made an impassioned speech explaining everything and he still rejected my reasoning. I despaired.

The session broke for lunch. Afterwards, the minister stopped me at the door and said: 'What did you say?'

I replied: 'You know what I said.'

He said: 'But what *did* you say?'

I said: 'It will be in *Hansard*.'

He said: 'Well, where's the *Hansard*?'

I said: '*Hansard* does not come out for a couple of days on Standing Committees. You know that. You've been here a lot longer than me.'

He said: 'You don't understand. My civil servants tell me that I have changed my mind and I must know what you said and why I changed it.'

Back in committee, he got up and said there had been consideration during the break and he was prepared to consider further and maybe the Member concerned (that was me) would have a meeting with his officials and we could take the matter forward. That was the breakthrough. The civil servants told me I had explained the point at issue in a way they had never heard before and at last they understood. This was a real victory, because the computer industry had been trying to explain it to the civil servants and the House of Lords (the first House to have a Science and Technology Committee) for years. A Green Paper – a discussion document – on the question of software protection had been out for ten years, but fatal flaws remained in the draft legislation which would have had the opposite effect to that intended, removing computer software from copyright protection in Britain instead of creating that protection.

I worked closely with the civil servants, and together we created the best copyright legislation for computer software in the world, contained in the Copyright, Designs and Patents Act 1988. The task was a difficult one, but the results repaid our efforts. Officials in the United States paid us the compliment of saying that our Act was as good as theirs. My own work in this area expanded. I developed close links with the Copyright Committee of the British Computer Society. I formed a large group of eminent people from the computer industry, including representatives of IBM and ICL. We worked hard with Brussels and brought in stronger legislation within the European Community, and then turned our efforts to the international scene and the Uruguay Round GATT agreement, in which the West traded copyright protection in the less developed world in return for greater fairness in agriculture. I advised various east European governments on the need to imple-ment software copyright. I talked with the Scientific Committee of the Japanese Parliament, and began discussions with China.

I then moved straight on to working on computer hacking, where further legislation was urgently needed. The sanctions against hacking I had been able to have included in the 1988 Act were very small, because hacking was seen as a civil and not a criminal trespass. So, with the assistance of the industry team I had assembled, I put together a top-class, really innovatory Computer Hacking Bill. I tried to get the Government to concentrate on it and couldn't. So I tabled 137 parliamentary questions to all the different departments and wrote an article for *The Times* pointing out the dangers of unprotected computer information. Somebody from the Ministry of Defence turned up at my house half an hour after breakfast, begging me not to write such truthful things again because it might give people ideas on how to hack into defence systems. I said I was only speculating. He said, 'Yes, but it's true. Please don't mention it again.' So I didn't.

I then had a visit from a judicial eminence from the Royal Navy who told me about a small piece of legislation which had already gone through on national security grounds relating to this sort of work. I thanked him and went to look up that Act because it gave a precedent. The next thing I knew was that Tom King, Secretary of State for Defence, had called and disciplined him for talking to a Member of Parliament. This was absurd, to try to stop a Member of Parliament learning from a serving officer about an already published Act of Parliament. I went in to see Tom King and asked for the ministry's support, subsequently briefing the ministry fully on my proposal.

After working very hard throughout the summer of 1990 to advance this legislation, in the face of other ministerial obstacles, I saw my Bill first redrafted by Government draftsmen and then, at the last moment, dropped. This happened because Lord Young was replaced as Secretary of State for Trade and Industry by Nicholas Ridley, who did not understand the issue. He discarded the carefully crafted legislation in favour of a small Bill, subsequently deemed valueless by other Members, from Douglas Hogg on something else.

Later that autumn I persuaded another Member to take the Bill up, in a very much weaker form, and put it forward as a Private Member's Bill, when he had the good fortune to strike lucky in the annual draws. I explained it all to him very carefully, but a Private Member's Bill is the target of anyone and everyone on a Friday morning who cares to knock it down. A minor version of it squeezed through, but very few prosecutions resulted. The expert Computer Crime Squad at Scotland Yard, with whom I had worked, was then disbanded and years of reduction in electronic crime were thrown away. Ministers simply were not sophisticated enough to understand that white-collar crime in the world of the Internet is just as corrupting as, and probably far vaster in financial consequence than, theft by masked robbers in high street banks.

I had to drop this work once I became a PPS in the Home Office; but my own interest in ownership of information and individuals' right to privacy grew, and I began intermittent discussions during my voluntary refugee education project with Dr Federico Mayor, Director-General of UNESCO, with whom I forged a close working partnership in 1993.

Among my fundamental objections to the poll tax – of which there were several – one related directly to my concern with computer security. Among its many flaws, it drew together about a citizen, on one form, knowledge about tax and savings, income and expenditure, which would be laid for rebate purposes before the local authority. Because I had initiated legislation on computer fraud, I knew full well that computers could be hacked into, and that this information would not be secure. I knew that the creation of security for computerized information required an investment of five times the cost of the hardware, and that local authorities had virtually no protection of any sort. Nor could they ever be expected to pay such sums. Most importantly of all, in our system tax and social welfare details had always traditionally been kept separate. The great danger of pulling all this information about each individual together was that it would give the state complete control over the individual. In other words, we were demolishing a long-held bulwark against state power without either understanding what we were doing or even having a debate on it in Parliament. I sent a leaflet to the Data Protection Registrar and bitterly complained to everyone that this would be a destruction of individual British human rights.

But the poll tax juggernaut rolled inexorably on, and I and my constituents learned the hard way that no confidence could be placed in Government statements, public or private. The Conservative Whip for the south-west MPs in the 1987 Parliament was a war hero from a Cornish family, Bob

Boscowen. I respected Bob deeply, but he did let me down over the poll tax. I pointed out to him in the second vote that the sum of money to be paid had gone up from one hundred pounds to over two hundred pounds and said that this was going too far. He assured me that if I continued to vote with the Government, he could guarantee it would go no higher. I voted accordingly, and was dismayed some months later to discover that the sum had indeed gone beyond that level. The poor were bound to suffer unless the payments were kept under a hundred-pound ceiling, as we were originally told they would be. And, without mandatory identity cards, how could an increasingly mobile population be forced to pay? (The possibility of identity cards was raised again later under Michael Howard's tenure as Home Secretary. In his world the information on the cards would belong to Government; for myself, unless that ownership rested with the individual, I could never do other than argue against such a scheme.) The £7 billion final bill to the taxpayer for the poll tax was a monument to ministerial ignorance and obduracy.

Ministers' political ignorance can be breathtaking. On Spanish access to our traditional fishing grounds, as with many other aspects of policy, the Conservatives have ended up fighting their own record. For, of course, the Conservatives were in government when Spain joined the EC. Ministers did not seem to realize until very late in the day that we had sold the pass on Spanish fishing rights in 1983. I saw how little ministers knew and how wrong civil servants were to assume that they knew even the ground rules of their topics. By June 1996 Tony Baldry, the fisheries minister, was declaring that 'UK fish are for UK fishermen', thus contradicting the very policy he was pushing in Brussels – and, moreover, displaying a touching faith in the willingness of fish to stay in one place and not swim away.

The issue of data protection and personal privacy showed me that the responsible ministers neither understood their briefs well enough to carry out their role competently nor grasped the impact of EU directives on national law. Right through the 1980s, Margaret Thatcher presided over a Government and party which seemed wilfully to misunderstand Britain's European commitments. As Lord Cockfield has shown in his book on the Single Market, this simply stored up trouble for the future:

> To some extent the paucity of information given to Parliament and the fact that it was so out of focus reflects the Prime Minister's own outlook and priorities. To some extent it is a reflection of a conviction unsupported by experience, that if you ignore something it will go away. But its legacy is to be seen today in an anti-European lobby whose ideas, whose approach and whose rhetoric is based on an extensive and fundamental lack of understanding of the facts.
>
> (*The European Union: Creating the Single Market*, 1994, p. 144)

Emphasizing the supposed legal status of a commitment rather than its content on more than one occasion, she adopted what Lord Cockfield calls 'the tax lawyers' outlook: not how to give effect to the intention of the Statute, but how to avoid it' (*Creating the Single Market*, p. 136).

Mrs Thatcher did not see Europe in the way that many of those who had fought saw it. Her folk memories promoted not the importance of peace but the perpetuation of enmity. Nicholas Ridley's anti-German sentiments found in her a ready audience; it was only the airing of them in public which cost him his office. From the outset she was anxious to take Europe on for domestic reasons. This is how Nicholas Ridley recalled the beginnings of the budget battle in his book '*My Style of Government': The Thatcher Years* (1991): 'It gave her a chance to be seen to be fighting publicly for British interests and to do battle with the Community on an issue unlikely to split the Party because it was not in any way concerned with sovereignty or the "European ideal"' (p. 138).

Where Margaret Thatcher differed from some of her prede-
cessors is that she, and some of those closest to her, sought to
explain away her actions, to deny their apparent purport.
Nicholas Ridley tied himself in terrible knots trying to explain
why a plain text could not have meant what it said. He wrote: 'It
was held against her later that we had accepted the principle [of
EMU] by agreeing to a Single European Act; an argument which
I believe to be fallacious, since it would only be true if Britain had
agreed to a directive bringing about EMU, which we would never
have done. After all, there had been many earlier declaratory
commitments to EMU by the EC' ('*My Style of Government*',
p. 143). On social policy, she has sought to disclaim the Madrid
communiqué of June 1989, agreed at the end of a summit which
she will surely never forget, which committed her to the view that
'in the construction of the single European market social aspects
should be given the same importance as economic aspects'. She
wrote later: 'I always considered that this meant the advantages
in terms of jobs and living standards which would flow from freer
trade' (*The Downing Street Years*, 1993, p. 751). During 1989 the
Department of Employment had been fighting a running propaganda battle against European social policy, particularly the
Social Charter. It is impossible to conclude from its publications
or from the Community's own proposals that action in the social
area was likely to be confined to watching the operation of
market forces in the single market.

The intergovernmental conference at Maastricht in 1990–1
provided the present Government with an opportunity to
produce its own critique of the Community's development.
Although France and Germany had the weightiest agendas for
that IGC, wishing to deal with the consequences of German
reunification, other member states saw action at the European
level as a valuable means of easing domestic pressure. The final
treaty also illustrated the member states' growing habit of
responding to unexpected judgments of the European Court by
making treaty amendments. There were clear signs that whatever

Margaret Thatcher and her ministers may now claim to have thought about 'declaratory' provisions, British negotiators understood very well the importance and value of a well-phrased preamble. John Major became Prime Minister in time to claim British elements of the treaty as his own. The overwhelming impression gained from looking at the British submissions to the Maastricht IGC in the light of subsequent events has nothing to do with any serious British critique of Europe. It is simply that the long-standing flaws in British policy became more obvious and more immediate under his leadership.

The Government made clear and positive proposals on the role of national parliaments, based upon an implicit recognition that all had not been well in the manner in which the Community's development had been communicated and explained to, or legitimized by, Europe's various parliamentarians. Reference was made to the need to improve relations between national parliaments and the European. John Major's overtures to the MEPs proved to be little more than window-dressing, however, and the same was true of Britain's proposals to the IGC. The border between irony and farce was finally crossed when it became clear that strenuous efforts had been made by the Government to prevent MPs from seeing its own draft declaration on providing better information for national parliaments. As for his views on the European Parliament, John Major trod an uncertain path back on to territory formerly occupied by his predecessor, who regarded the Strasbourg assembly with a visceral loathing. In the course of his William and Mary lecture 'Europe: A Future that Works', delivered in Leiden on 7 September 1994, he abandoned all idea of the Community's legitimacy resting on twin pillars of national and European parliaments, as set out in a Government note of 1991 on the *Role of National Parliaments in the European Community*, and stated instead that the EU derives 'its basic democratic legitimacy through the national Parliaments', adding, 'That should remain the case.'

The Conservative election manifesto of 1992 declared that 'The Conservative Party has been the Party of Europe for thirty years . . . We have not wavered nor changed our views.' The reality is very different.

When John Redwood now complains that 'Europe does have direct and real power over our lives . . . it can lose you your job; it has plans to transform the way we are governed' ('How we can use beef to beat Kohl', *The Times*, 24 May 1996), one can look back to the comments of Lords Dilhorne and Kilmuir and see, at a stroke, how it is that the most considered attempt ever made at the avoidance of war has itself become a focus of resentment, in Britain at least. I may appear to be making the sceptics' case for them, but I am not. Their route to Britain's salvation consists of disastrous adjustments in her foreign relations. I see the British *pas devant les enfants* technique, employed so often by Europe's supporters in government, most of whom have been in the Conservative Party, as the root cause of our problems with Europe. Beyond that, I see any political system which facilitates misconception and frustrates democratic legitimacy on this scale as long overdue for reform.

As the poll tax debate deepened and my work on copyright issues continued, I was also working on data protection legislation which was coming out of Brussels. There was already a Data Protection Act of 1984 which was a skeleton version of a Bill put forward originally by the Council of Europe and adopted by the European Union; but that legislation did not really do very much for the United Kingdom because Mrs Thatcher's Government was unwilling to implement it properly. People badly needed protection of information about them held by other people on computer.

Britain's scrutiny of the European legislation was sadly lacking. The responsible minister in the Home Office did not understand the issues; in committee she told me that I knew a lot more about it than she did. Dealing with complex legislation demands a minister who has sufficient intellectual grasp or specialist expertise to cope. This we did not have. The new European data protection legislation was a carbon copy of the Data Protection Act of Stuttgart in Germany. Clearly, what suited the citizens of Stuttgart was not right for the citizens of the United Kingdom. A series of industrialists and bankers came to see me because I was in Parliament and known to be knowledgeable about computers. I went straight round to the Home Office to point out to another minister that this new legislation was contrary to certain sections of our Copyright Act. He said that my points were of no consequence even if I were correct, because our Copyright Act stood supreme. I pointed out that this was not so and that this new legislation would overlay and not be subsumed by our Copyright Act. The minister and the civil servants told me I did not understand: our Copyright Act would incorporate this new Data Protection Directive once it was agreed, and would dissolve the parts that were not the same. I insisted this was not correct. The European legislation would overwhelm our own, and those strenuously argued parts of the Copyright Act which were in conflict with this new data protection legislation would be lost. They assured me I was wrong. Months later they found out that I was right; and, of course, as I told them at the time, that this applied to all incoming European legislation. It is astonishing that the Government did not understand this and its enormous implications, so long after the Treaty of Rome and the Single European Act.

Of course, information by itself is not enough, although it is the essential prerequisite of an informed debate. But over and above a grasp of the facts, what the Conservative Party had lacked, since Heath's departure from the leadership, was some grand oratory to sweep the European case along and help the British people to understand why our continuing membership of this, the largest market in the entire world, was so essential and why, if any single market is to survive, some properly enforced regulations are necessary to protect the weak against

Chapter 8

An Exercise of Judgement

In autumn 1989, I was struggling to get across to Mrs Thatcher the view that married non-working women should be allowed a poll-tax rebate. I had a long, arduous fight with her on this point, and totally failed to convince her of the justice of my case. In my view either it had to be won or the poll tax had to be thrown out, because these women did not have any income from which to pay another tax. In my constituency the poll tax was allowed to rise to upwards of four hundred pounds per person. This faced a young married couple with poll tax bills of nearly a thousand pounds on their income after tax. Yet our two district councils were models of efficiency and economy of style. I told Mrs Thatcher that local salaries were very low. A young man might be earning a wage of just over five thousand pounds a year, just above the cut-off point for a poll-tax rebate for him. She was breaking marriages up. Was this what she intended? Her reply was that I did not understand the purpose of marriage, what it was for. It was the role of the husband to take care of his wife, which included the duty to pay the bills. I answered that this was a tax against the wife, which she has to pay. I pointed out that if the husband were to pay his wife's poll tax, then his tax would be doubled and the wife would pay nothing, which was even more nonsensical. After all, her stated justification for this tax was individual responsibility. It was no use.

In March 1990, I had two informal meetings with her, in which I pleaded my case again. When she would not or could not understand the need for the reform, I found myself turning away from her, politically as well as personally, for the first time ever. Mrs Thatcher had given me the responsibility of looking at women's issues, and I had accepted it. I could not duck the task when the going got rough – as it had over independent taxation for married women. Domestically, it was the harshness of the poll tax system on non-working married women which made me throw in my hand so far as she was concerned. Internationally, it was the dreadful realization that she opposed the most important goal of all, the greatest and most welcome change, the reunification of Germany and the opening up of central and eastern Europe and beyond.

It was not clear precisely why she opposed Germany unity. She had passed the Single European Act, got it through on a whisker with virtually no debate. There we were, coming up towards this peaceful, triumphant conclusion to the Cold War; and just when the reunification of Germany became a likely outcome, she supported Nicholas Ridley's anti-German views, as expressed in an article in the *Spectator* magazine written by Nigel Lawson's son, Dominic. The article caused a furore in the Conservative Party and the Whips came round asking colleagues if Nicholas Ridley should stay on as a Government minister. I said no, he should go. But Mrs Thatcher would not sack him; eventually, the party had to force his resignation. Refusal to get rid of him amounted to her endorsement of his views. I could not follow a leader who opposed the reunification of Germany. For myself as for so many others, Germany's reunion was the key to the dissolution of the Soviet bloc and thus to the future peace and prosperity of Europe.

I had tracked Margaret Thatcher's philosophy carefully from the time she took over from Ted Heath. I applauded when she said to the party conference in Blackpool in 1975 that 'They [the communists] are not prosperous as we in the West are prosperous, and they are not free as we in the West are free,' and 'Our capitalist system produces a far higher standard of prosperity and happiness because it believes in incentive and opportunity and because it is founded on human dignity and freedom.' She always said to me: 'Freedom is the goal, Emma.' Now, having been her Party Vice-Chairman, personally working towards the achievement of our declared central goal of freedom, I saw that she had walked away from her own views. When it came to the crunch, she did not want freedom for everyone, as I did: not, in any event, for the people of East Germany, or for the people of West Devon; not economic freedom for young married women who could not find a paid job, or perhaps did not want to because they had young families or elderly relatives to care for.

The people of eastern Germany, Poland and Hungary had a claim on my loyalty. I remembered their refugees sheltering in Britain in the post-war years. As a child at the time of the Hungarian Revolution, I remember my father working so hard to reunite families there. How could I not fight for these people? That had been her goal too, the restoration of their freedom. And she lost it. She ran into the sand. She was leader too long.

In autumn 1989 Sir Anthony Meyer, as a keen supporter of the European Union, put his name forward to stand against Mrs Thatcher for the position of party leader. The rules brought in by the Conservative Party providing for the election of their leader (instead of 'emergence' by Establishment osmosis) had been drafted by Humphrey Berkeley. Humphrey had crossed the floor of the House not once but twice, and during his peregrinations had come to the conclusion that some form of voting system would be better for democracy than first past the post. Also in the spirit of democracy, he and his colleagues in the Conservative Party accepted that the party should have the opportunity to hold a leadership election every year, in November. Most newer members, myself included, were wholly unaware of this provision.

Sir Anthony Meyer put his name forward as a 'stalking horse', making it plain that he anticipated no great vote in his favour but hoping to enable a stronger candidate against Mrs Thatcher to emerge. Later I understood that this could have been someone such as Sir Ian Gilmour (a former minister sacked by Mrs Thatcher). In the end, only Sir Anthony was willing to go through with the plan. It cost him dear. The Conservative press, presumably tipped off by the Whips, unravelled his private life. He was preserved by his dignity, together with the sweet nature of his loving wife. In the public eye they emerged with strength and honour after a gruelling election phase. Mrs Thatcher, in America after the vote was settled, said prophetically: 'Yes, but what happens next year?'

The winter passed, dominated politically by the poll tax, its exceptional unfairness uppermost in the public mind and civil disorder breaking out. In April 1990, I made my public stand on the matter. I took a BBC camera team from *On the Record* and allowed them to film the iniquity of the poll tax as it applied in my constituency. I said:

> The Community Charge is riddled with unfairness and inconsistencies. These impact on me through my constituents. If I take the case of [a couple] who live out in the wilds of Dartmoor very happily – they have no made-up road, no electricity, no water, by their own choice – that blows into infinity the fiction that the Community Charge is related to the services you are deemed to use. That is just one unfairness; there are far too many as deep and fundamental as that.

It was later in 1990 that Nicholas Ridley made his views on Germany clear and Mrs Thatcher, by refusing to sack him, did likewise. The other half of my decision was made. Internationally, she had lost her footing; I could not follow her there. Domestically her touch had gone as well. She could no longer be my leader. November came and, after much shilly-shallying, Michael Heseltine took the plunge and put his name forward as a contender for the leadership – to my surprise, as he had said publicly that he would not oppose Mrs Thatcher for the post. The following day he approached me in the Lobby and asked me for my support. I told him it was probable that he had it, but that I was going to consult in my constituency before I finally decided. Frankly, I would have voted for any one of half a dozen people had they stood, among them Kenneth Clarke, Douglas Hurd, Nigel Lawson, Ted Heath (alas, his age seemed to debar him from another attempt at the leadership) and other second-rank runners such as Malcolm Rifkind. But Michael Heseltine had been the only one to step forward.

Our system can be tragic in its effects. Margaret Thatcher should have gone after ten years, as she was requested to do. She should never have put herself through that final set of hoops. The crunch should never have come in the way in which it did. I felt saddened that the all-powerful ministerial triumvirate of Lawson, Hurd and Howe, the Chancellor, Home Secretary and Foreign Secretary, had not acted sooner and forced her to resign. They could have done so, and in doing so would have avoided most of the pain and all of the blood that subsequently lay on the floor and stained the Conservative Party for years. For all of those three knew the score. Had they come together and gone in to see her, she would have had to give in and go. As it was, Geoffrey Howe acted alone and his resignation speech pulled out the base of the house of cards. It tumbled rapidly thereafter.

I had told Michael Heseltine that I would have to consult my constituency before I could confirm my support for him. The Humphrey Berkeley rules allowed several weeks for such consultations; Mrs Thatcher, however, perhaps ill advised by her PPS, Charlie Morrison's brother Peter, or her campaign managers, headed by Gerry Neale, the Member for Cornwall North, allowed no time to ponder or to consult. A rapid circuit of soundings was taken by the party among MEPs, in accordance with the rules, as was a whip-round of the House of Lords, and anyone who expressed a wish to consult with those who really counted was given short shrift. But I knew that I had to talk to my constituents. After all, it was in order to lift the poll tax off their backs that I was prepared to act. I needed to seek the views of my constituency Conservative association, my local friends and colleagues. I already knew what my constituents as a whole would like to happen: over the past few months I had received over four thousand letters against the poll tax. My constituents, along with most of the electorate, found this method of tax-gathering abhorrent. The early trickle of complaint in the days when it had been mooted at one hundred pounds a head had turned into a torrent, and with the local bill now running at four hundred pounds a head in an area of low incomes my postbag was likely to remain large.

The chips were down by Wednesday night. On Thursday morning, to my surprise, I was approached by Gerry Neale, who asked me to front Mrs Thatcher's campaign on television. I was astounded. Surely he had known about my opposition to her, both on Germany and on the poll tax, which I had after all made very plain? I said no, I thought it was unlikely that I could support her, though I did not yet know whether I would oppose her. He looked shocked and moved on. Very puzzled, I felt it essential that I let Number Ten know that I could not support the Prime Minister and might abstain, or even vote against her.

I sought out an old friend, Brian Griffiths, then head of the PM's Downing Street team. We had a shared history in the constituency of Blyth, where he had stood for the Conservatives in both 1974 elections before I was selected for the seat. More recently, in 1990 he and I had worked together to set up a small but effective charity called Cities in the Schools which aimed to seek out and redirect persistent truants in inner-city areas. Both of us had seen the particular system work uniquely well in the United States, and had separately determined to create a British copy. I found Brian at a media party, as I guessed I would, and told him that I could not support Mrs Thatcher and wanted her to know this. He looked at me seriously and asked: 'Are you telling me that this election actually matters?'

'Yes,' I said. 'Doesn't anyone in Number Ten realize this is for real?'

He said: 'I am not sure that we do. But thank you for telling me. Perhaps I should look for another job.' I told him that in my opinion he should. Now at least I had made my position clear to the party establishment

Very troubled, I went down the following morning to my constituency. The BBC team called and I allowed them to turn up on Saturday to film me consulting with my constituents. I called a meeting of the Stowford Branch, not knowing what they would think. The branch chairman, an elderly farmer, Lil Vigers, declared, 'She'm got to go.' Others got in touch with me from Tavistock, where Michael Heseltine had been Member of Parliament for nine years. Some said they had marked him down as a future Prime Minister, and urged me to support him rather than abstain. A member of that earlier selection committee sounded a note of caution: wonderful though she had found him, she was not sure he was prime ministerial material. But she was the only one. I went to another branch meeting that evening. Finally, at an early Christmas dinner in South Zeal village, I found myself beside the chairman of the constituency association, Geoffrey Cleverdon. The branch concerned could not get the village hall later in December and we were surrounded by crackers and paper hats, with waiters and waitresses in attendance. By the time we had finished dinner, I was left with the impression that how I cast my leadership vote was up to me. As far as he was concerned I could vote any way I liked.

On Monday lunchtime the BBC team caught up with me again. I had agreed that I would make my decision after thorough canvassing in the constituency and would let them know for the one o'clock news. That way, the constituency would know my decision before I voted; with so little time allowed for consultation – by Mrs Thatcher's choice – the media was the only channel through which I could inform them all. No more than five minutes before we were due to go on air,

I received an urgent message to call John Gummer and talk to him about my leadership vote. It appeared to me that John wanted to influence my decision for one reason or another. The news programme was already running. I was in the interviewee's chair. I could not stop everything for John Gummer. If it was an agricultural matter (he was minister of agriculture) or any other parliamentary business, the call could wait five minutes. If it was to do with Mrs Thatcher, well, my choice might not be his. But he did not own my vote. I made a clear statement on the one o'clock news that, in line with the wishes of my constituents, I could not support Mrs Thatcher and I had decided to support Michael Heseltine, who had put his name forward and who had the support of Tavistock, his former seat. It took just a few minutes. Then I went to the telephone. John Gummer did not take my call. The battle lines had been drawn.

I subsequently discovered that on the previous day, the Sunday, Conservative Central Office had assumed a proactive role on Mrs Thatcher's behalf. Originally, they had stood aside when the Thatcher–Heseltine boxing match began. Suddenly, all this had changed.

Immediately after the one o'clock news bulletin on Monday my constituency chairman and local party agent called press conferences and criticized the stand I had taken, apparently distancing themselves from me. I was astonished, as I had understood the chairman had given me a free rein only a few days earlier. The next day the party chairman was on the *Nine o'Clock News* claiming that he had told me to vote for Mrs Thatcher, but I have no recollection of this being said in our conversation. Before casting my vote I had polled each member of the constituency's finance and general purposes committee most carefully and kept the notes. Eight out of ten at that time said they were against her, and of the other two, only one asked me to abstain. It seemed to me that the chairman's comments were out of step with the views of senior constituency officials.

On Wednesday evening, after continuing declarations, I cleared my conscience with a real *éminence grise*. To my surprise, he responded that it was time for Mrs Thatcher to go. It had been decided, he added ominously. Her resignation the following day came to me as no surprise.

For days a battle royal raged on the *Nine o'Clock News* and *News at Ten*. I reiterated that I had made my decision after consulting first the Conservative association and its branches and also the wider constituency at large; my constituency chairman and agent stuck to the story that they had told me to support Mrs Thatcher and that I had disobeyed them. This misunderstanding was to continue to dog my relationship with the constituency chairman and agent. Even a year later, the agent, through the newsletter of the South West Group of the Agents' Association, was continuing to criticize me – in my view significantly undermining the Conservative position and possibly damaging me in the constituency.

I still have a note I made at the time to help me order my own thoughts on the reasons for backing Michael Heseltine. Such notes are vital when facing impromptu media interviews day after day. I wrote that to vote for Heseltine was 'to accept that recently the Prime Minister has too personally dominated the Cabinet and the Government. The British people are averse to power [being] concentrated in hands that are getting inflexible.'

In the House of Commons, my declaration resulted in the unexpected opening of a door into the underground warren containing Heseltine's secret support army. I was astounded to find how effective and well advanced their plans had been, and for how long. His campaign leaders filled me in, saying quite rightly that as I had stood up for their cause, I should be co-opted into the team. The picture changed dramatically with Mrs Thatcher's withdrawal after the first vote, becoming more fluid as three figures emerged to contest the second ballot: Douglas Hurd, whom I should have supported but to whom I felt unable to switch my allegiance, having already declared myself so strongly for Heseltine; John Major, whom I would never have supported – I could not see how someone without clear leadership qualities was going to be able to keep the Conservative Party together after such a strong leader as Thatcher; and Michael Heseltine, to whose cause I was by then inevitably welded. He lost. I asked him for a job. Could I be his Parliamentary Private Secretary? I was on the brink of deselection in the constituency, and I would have loved the job. Of all his supporters, perhaps I had stretched myself furthest for him. He rejected my offer curtly and I never asked him for a job again. That was in 1990.

The Conservative Government in power in the 1990s was marked by an almost total lack of leadership. The results of this were just the same as in any organization: cohesion unravelled, groups and factions sprang up – of which the anti-Europeans, led by Bill Cash, were one of the more prominent – and the official work of the Conservative parliamentary party, that carried out by the ministers, became semi-detached. Individual departments ambled in various directions, for the lack of leadership arose first from a lack of vision, of any clear picture of where the Conservative Party wished to lead the nation, even of why it was in power at all. Thus the departmental ministers fell back on trying to make their departments run as effectively as possible (a job best left to the civil servants and fully trained political commissioners); sometimes they were so career-driven that the civil servants themselves were forced into a more political position. As I moved through the various ministries I saw that ministers were taking executive decisions rather than policy ones, and walking right over the old divide between ministers, deciding policy, and civil servants, executing it. Nor was there any unified approach that the ministers could adopt, since the unity of a team can only come from the team leader. When Gillian Shephard had stopped me in the Members' cloakroom the day before the last leadership vote in 1990 and begged me to support John Major, I told her frankly that I did not believe that he had the leadership qualities required. I wished that I had been proved wrong.

The demand for good leadership was all the greater because of the number of ministerial posts created by Margaret Thatcher. Managing an over-large team calls for the highest-quality managerial and leadership skills: keeping people highly motivated and active, with sufficient real work to do, is one of the most difficult tasks. John Major couldn't do it. Margaret Thatcher did it, and also – at least in the earlier years of her leadership – kept many backbenchers involved as well, by setting up working groups on every conceivable issue as elections approached. She kept ministers on their toes and the whole of the parliamentary party occupied by pushing through an unprecedented weight of legislation, demanding full voting turnouts on even the most minor issues. The hours were dreadful, but she achieved her goal: a finely tuned, alert party of MPs, knowledgeable and committed, working if not to her goals then at least to a parliamentary goal.

John Major came in, the temperature dropped, the pace slackened, the water stilled, and since then we have paddled in a stagnant pond.

Down in the constituency, the row went on. The Exeter-based Conservative Central Office senior agent, Bill Henderson, told me brusquely that in the last resort his job was to keep a Conservative Member of Parliament in the seat. He put a little weight into the situation and the threat of deselection passed at a complex and difficult meeting just before Christmas. A comment often repeated subsequently by the party, both locally and nationally, was that since I was the only person who could hold the seat of Devon West and Torridge against the Liberal Democrats, I had to be kept on.

Chapter 9

The Balance Tilts

During the months and years following the Conservative leadership election of 1990 my life changed markedly and permanently. Some of the changes were personal. But for a politician, personal experiences can bring greater wisdom for use in the public world. As a result of the Gulf War I took on a series of new, large responsibilities for others in need. These choices heightened and sharpened my knowledge of the impact of the Government's policies, particularly on parents, patients in hospitals, doctors, surgeons, nurses, schoolboys and teachers, refugees and the law. For reasons of policy and principle I should have left the Conservative Party earlier than I did. Personal ties bound me; but in the end ordinary people's pain and despair freed me to act, for them.

Saddened by the destruction in Iraq as well as in Kuwait, I pointed out, in a parliamentary question, that once the Gulf War was over, when of course the world would help Kuwait to rebuild itself as fast as possible, help would also be needed for the victims inside Iraq. Could we not assist them too? After the end of the war I went to help the Iraqi victims, both those within Iraq in the southern marshlands and those who had fled across the border to seek safety inside Iran. This work continues today. I repeatedly raised the issue of Saddam Hussein's draining of the marshes in southern Iraq. Many thousands of Iraqi people were affected, and an entire way of life was being deliberately destroyed. Douglas Hogg gave me the impression that he did not want me to run with this issue. He, of course, would have known from RAF reconnaissance that the marshlands were being destroyed and should have been under no illusion about the scale of the disaster. If the British public knew what was going on, there would be pressure placed upon him to do something about it.

Saddam Hussein deceived the Gulf States as well as the West. Thirty-six hours before he invaded Kuwait he was welcoming the Emir of that country in Baghdad, assuring him of his eternal fidelity and calling him 'my brother'. So confident was Kuwait of the friendship of Iraq that the Emir even offered Saddam the task of looking after his son and heir if anything happened to the Emir himself. Why did the Iraqi people allow a man of Saddam's cruelty to rise to the leadership? And how is it that so many Iraqi people have participated in some of the cruellest forms of torture and murder ever devised? It is true to say that this regime is one of the most brutal ever known. It is a terrible regime, exercised by a brutalized people. As in Nazi Germany, it had become impossible to draw clear distinctions between the damned and damning, the tortured and the torturers, the executed and the executioners. I had firm evidence of this, not just from the stories of torture given to me by heartbroken and physically broken men and women in the refugee camps of southern Iran and across the borders in the vanishing marshes of Iraq. I also have letters from prisoners in the depths of dungeons inside Iraq detailing the inhuman treatments they were experiencing. I doubt many of the authors are now alive, although they wrote to me only two years ago.

Perhaps the West's ambivalent treatment of Iraq had exacerbated the Iraqis' maltreatment of themselves and others. In the Iran–Iraq War Britain, in common with thirty-seven other nations, sold arms to both sides. Apparently Britain didn't care that over a million young men, volunteers and conscripts alike, and thousands of civilian families suffered death and destruction as a direct result. Only in 1993 did the United Nations, with Britain a Permanent Member of the Security Council, acknowledge what everyone should long have known, namely that Iraq, and not the Islamic Republic of Iran, was the aggressor. Immediately after the end of the war, just days after its withdrawal from southern Iran, the remnants of the Iraqi army, equipped with chemical weapons, were directed by Saddam Hussein against the Iraqi Kurds. Yet even that terrible offensive did not seem to convince the British Government of the need to support the Iraqi people. The now famous guidelines on the sales of armaments to Iraq, drawn up by minister Richard Luce in 1983 and put to the House of Commons by the then Foreign Secretary Geoffrey Howe in 1985, were decisively cast aside after Geoffrey Howe had left the Foreign Office. Yet William Waldegrave subsequently told the House of Commons that the guidelines both remained unchanged and were not being breached. With human lives at stake, can ignorance ever be any political defence? I think not. It is the duty of the Government to take responsibility for governing, and to equip itself with all the information required before making definitive statements of that nature within a democratic society such as the United Kingdom.

The Iraqi people cannot duck some element of responsibility for choosing Saddam as their leader, for allowing such evil and corrupt people to rise to the surface like scum on a stinking pond. But the people I was assisting inside and outside the Iraqi marshlands bore no taint of guilt. There could be no justification for the treatment that they were receiving. They were peaceful people, aquaculturalists, direct descendants of the Sumerians who had invented the wheel, converted hieroglyphics into writing in 4,000 BC and developed the concept of the rule of law and civil cooperation, subsequently taken up by the ancient Greeks. Other people, too, were standing up to Saddam, educated and professional people; doctors, nurses, teachers, merchants and owners of small businesses based in the cities around the marshlands. The names of those cities had great resonance: Basra, Najaf, the great Holy City of Islam, al-Amarah. They may have post-dated the cities of Babylon and Ur, but the people's roots went back that far. Now their nominal national leader was doing his best to wipe them out. The sight first of starving clusters of refugees in close earshot of the Iraqi army's front line deep in the marshlands, their historic ways of life destroyed, and then of thousands flooding across the border into Iran, provoked in me a reaction of deep sorrow. The political situation was beyond me; but perhaps it would be possible to offer practical help. I set up the AMAR Appeal.

My aim was humanitarian; I was not setting myself up to second-guess the world's diplomats. Douglas Hurd was immediately supportive. So were Paddy Ashdown and Speaker Weatherall; and then John Smith, John Major, Lynda Chalker, Dale Campbell-Savours and many more. Others were not. They were hostile, I think, because I worked, and continue to work, in partnership with Iran and the Iranian people. The barbarism of the Shah's secret police, the Rushdie affair and other atrocities have clouded the West's perception of Iran; but by contrast with the West and its regional neighbours, Iran accepts large numbers of refugees. I have found it easy to make friends at all levels of Iranian society. Despite the inevitable bias against English-speakers, born out of the bitterness still felt about the policies of the US Carter administration, the purpose of my work has been accepted by almost all Iranians I have met. Over one million miserable people in Iraq and Iran have benefited from the provision of clothing, shelter, clean water, primary health care, teaching and work. Ninety thousand refugees form the current most welcome workload and the work of the AMAR Appeal has now spread into Lebanon, Bosnia, Palestine and northern Iraq. I brought Amar himself, with forty-five per cent third degree burns, to Guy's Hospital in London and subsequently into our home.

Taking Amar into our family brought me right up against the effects of Government policies on health, social services, education, abused children, Care in the Community, the drug culture and local crime. I saw more sharply than ever before how substantially, even fundamentally, the reality of life on the ground differed from the scene as viewed from the top where policies were designed and proclaimed.

Take the policy of Care in the Community, intended to bring the mentally ill out of hospitals and into the ordinary world. In the mental health world it is always the patients who suffer. The architects of this policy failed to realize that public feeling about mental illnesses such as schizophrenia, and about the people who suffer from them, is still rooted in a primitive fear that these diseases, like others, may be catching. Not for nothing were the old mental hospitals built miles away from human habitation. Children with mental handicap have even been discarded by their parents. In the 1970s I frequently visited the home for mentally handicapped children within my father's region. Staff there constantly told us that they were lucky if some parents visited once a year. At least the older, local hospital boards, made up wholly of volunteers, brought some people from the local community into the mental hospitals and formed a link between the patients and the community. But the local government reform of 1974 was accompanied by the closure of these boards and the reorganization of their functions; and, as with the local elected councils, the reform resulted in new organizations that are more distant. Their members are paid, not volunteers, and are appointed by the Secretary of State for Health, ensuring a majority of Government supporters.

In the community care programme of the 1990s the Conservative Government failed the mentally ill again. The principle seemed sound, and for most patients care in the community was the right and proper way forward. But, as I said to successive health ministers, it would cost five times as much to look after a patient effectively in the community as in a long-stay hospital. On top of that, I felt that significant community education had to take place. Neither has happened. Instead, the Government has scrimped on both money and effort. In my own constituency even the councillors themselves voted against using a house in the best street in one of the market towns as a small home for mentally ill patients within the Care in the Community programme. People are frightened; they fear for their children's safety – and, since too little money has been put into policy's implementation to employ the necessary numbers of caring staff, perhaps they are right to do so. With insufficient resources being provided for proper care, a wretched cottage industry has grown up of small-scale, inadequately monitored accommodation for mental health patients. These provide a delectable continuing source of income for owners whose aim is to incur as little work for themselves as possible while charging the local authority for bedrooms for former hospital patients. The patients are wonderful trade; and scant checks are required by Government guidelines, particularly if you take in just a few. Yet the attention so badly needed is not being given. These are sick people; how can we justify this denial of care?

Nor have the needs of the acutely mentally ill been properly recognized. Long-stay beds have been cut below the necessary minimum, leaving the general population vulnerable to the uncontrollable emotions of the seriously disturbed. Some people need long-stay care even if not sick enough to be restricted by a legal order. The physical health needs of the mentally ill outside the hospital environment are not met. A major effort within my constituency by some dedicated local doctors and psychologists found that 40 per cent of the acutely mentally ill in their care had significant physical health problems (such as infected teeth), and that once these had been treated the patients were able to moderate their behaviour dramatically and for the good. Yet these patients' results were not picked up and copied for others. Care in the Community started to become a policy of less care for patients and more fear for the community.

A similar harshness on the part of Government was clear in respect of prisons. There were no women prisoners in

Dartmoor, but as a Howard League member I knew I had to visit their gaols. I went to Holloway and as a result put down a range of parliamentary questions in 1989 and 1990 on women in prison who were pregnant and had miscarried, or had had still-births, or had been returned to their cells straight after delivery in hospital. The answers were not satisfactory. I sought to find out what proportion of pregnancies in women prisoners had resulted in a miscarriage in the last ten years. The answer? The figure could not be given because the cost would be disproportionate. I asked about still-births to women prisoners; again a 'disproportionate cost' part-answer was returned. I did discover the numbers of those who had been sentenced to prison while pregnant. I continued my campaign.

It was through persistent questioning of Government ministers on matters such as these that it became clear to me that the Government deliberately withheld innocuous, basic knowledge from Members of Parliament. For example, during 1989 and 1990 I campaigned for improved safety standards on the buses and coaches on which children travelled to and from school. In December 1989 I tabled a parliamentary question asking how many children of school age had been injured or killed in traffic accidents involving designated school buses in the preceding twelve months; the answer was a bald: 'The information requested is not available.' It was only when, months later, I discovered from a friendly Civil Service source that the data to which I sought access did not specifically identify 'designated' school buses that I was able, by very slightly rewording the question to refer to 'bus or coach accidents while on a journey to and from school', to elicit columns of statistics.

I was particularly concerned about the misuse of medical information. Some years ago doctors began to be targeted by the drugs companies, who offered them cut-price computers in return for a consistent supply of details of patients – albeit not by name – so that the use of and reactions to drugs by doctors and patients could be monitored by the pharmaceutical companies and used to market their products to doctors more effectively. Of course, the key data which only the doctors held and which under this arrangement they were contracted to put on the computer for the companies came from the patients' records, hitherto kept on paper but now transferred to the new computers. Gradually, the GPs linked up their computers to share medical knowledge; then the GPs' computers were linked up with those of the hospitals. There is a very high level of error in the transfer of data on to computer by hospitals, and as the areas link into the region, and the regions coalesce in a national system, so access to everyone's medical record becomes possible by various routes, and errors abound and multiply.

Who owns the records? That is my concern. I don't want the citizen's privacy blown open like this. Nor do I want citizens to be exposed to blackmail, which frequently happens, and possibly harmed by medical knowledge being made available to the wrong people. So I put down a range of questions to the Secretary of State for Health, Virginia Bottomley: she then called in a Treasury QC who gave a holding ruling that the Government, represented in this case by the Secretary of State for Health, owned all medical records. I disputed this and continue to do so.

Doctors are not prevented by the Hippocratic Oath from divulging information to the drugs companies. In fact, many doctors today don't swear the Hippocratic Oath; it has gone out of fashion. Nor do they have any inhibitions about such disclosure. The truth of the matter is that the patient is not protected. Doctors needed computers. The NHS could not provide the extra money for them and the doctors could not afford to pay the bills themselves. So the drug companies jumped in, and as a result patients' privacy has been blown to smithereens.

Modern records contain an enormously varied spread of information about the patient. In the debate on the Access to Medical Records Bill, I made a speech pointing out that a GP is now entitled, and expects, to go to an astounding variety of people to get information about patients – teachers, police, social workers and other family members can all be approached for information without the patient seeing the subsequent record. I did co-sponsor a small piece of legislation to allow patients to fact-check the basic data of name and address; but the medical profession would not allow much more than that. I believe that is an impertinence, as is the claim of state owner-ship of the knowledge contained in the record about the patient. Each patient should have ownership of his or her own records. My primary concern was not purely about access to information for citizens, but about who owned the information. Access to information is certainly a big step forward; but it is insufficient to protect the citizen from an all-powerful state. I am delighted that the Labour Party has now followed the Liberal Democrats in accepting the need for freedom of information, a code phrase for access.

Failing to break that impasse between myself and the Government I turned to another sector: employment. In 1990 I drafted and put forward a Bill on access to information for employees. In the process I discovered just how deep the culture of using secretly collected and stored information on others against them had gone.

I was called in by the Whips. This felt rather like being a victim of official bullies at school might feel. In the Whips' Room were eight men, sitting or lounging in their chairs. Not one offered me a seat; I was left standing, no doubt on purpose. Led by the Chief Whip, Richard Ryder, they attacked me for about fifteen minutes. I had always heard that the Conservative Whips' Office was a place where higher human values were suspended. The Whips spent considerable amounts of time trying to discover things about backbenchers which could subsequently be used against them – as I found out when I voted against Mrs Thatcher in the leadership election of 1990. The Whips' Office is divided into areas, with a Whip allocated to each. The Whip has to come from that particular part of the United Kingdom, and is tasked with getting to know his members very well indeed so that any possible backsliding can be nipped in the bud before it has a chance to be expressed in an adverse vote.

On this occasion the Whips seemed particularly angry. As I listened, I realized that the Conservative Party had long held records on political activists of all kinds, especially those of extreme left-wing views. The list was being held by Dr Julian Lewis of the Conservative Research Department, a very able right-winger who in 1995 was selected as a Conservative Prospective Parliamentary Candidate. I tried to deflect the Whips' wrath through diversionary questions. I suggested that he should register his list with the Data Protection Registrar and comply with the law. They told me that he evaded the data protection legislation because Conservative Central Office kept nothing of this sort on computer. Any Bill such as that I was promoting would nullify his work as it embraced paper records. I argued that employees must have access to information held on them on paper files so that they could check that it was correct and not being used wrongly against them. I pointed out that my work on computerized information had made me understand that much of the danger of information held on individuals arises from inaccuracy. The Whips made it clear that their concern was not with accuracy but with secrecy. I thought of the similar file held in the Whips' Office on Members of Parliament. How could they be sure their own files weren't similarly unreliable? If they weren't sure, why were they wasting their money? Apart from the morality of the matter (my own deep concern), the files were in a mess. I told the Whips I thought they were being conned. 'Ah,' they said, 'we get it free.' What was the point of having information that was unreliable?, I asked. I told them I could let them know of reliable, blue-chip companies who could give them top-class accurate information on individuals if they really needed it, and within the law. But they did not want to pay the price of accuracy. Better free misinformation than a correct, paid-for file. And provided my Bill was quashed (which they could ensure), no one could inspect their records to verify the accuracy of the data. The ownership of their flawed records would rest with them.

Conservatives talk a lot about freedom for the individual, freedom from state control. But a critical freedom is under threat: freedom from others, particularly state servants, owning knowledge personal to you and thus forecasting your movements and foreclosing your options. Under Conservative Governments in recent years control over the individual has become stronger and more powerful than any of our forebears would have dreamed. The Conservative Party and Government which have preached against state control are in fact the worst culprits in exercising it.

In the Government's remorseless drive for the centralization of power and control, local government has been weakened beyond recognition. The ground was laid for the undermining of local autonomy by the Keith Joseph/Peter Walker reforms of 1974, for the new structures created a centralized system which allowed the government to take control of what had previously lain within the remit of local councillors. Today, most local government expenditure now either comes from or is strictly controlled by central government. The remainder is virtually all subject to stringent Government 'guidelines' – that is to say, rules devised in Whitehall to be implemented in hamlets, villages, towns and cities from one end of the country to the other. The individuality of local initiative has been snuffed out. In December 1995, after a meeting between ministers and local government representatives, the chief executive of one local council remarked to me that it had been wise not to bring councillors with him, since they now played no part in local government decisions and merely got in the way of the smooth implementation of central government's commands. They really had no place in local government other than window dressing.

Parallel to this remorseless containment of local government independence by the Conservative Government came the political colouring of public appointments on local boards. I was in Central Office when that change took place. Pressure came from local constituency people, who, seeing the growth of Government appointments, begged that these should not be filled by known Labour supporters. Of course, before Mrs Thatcher, most Government appointees were non-political figures anyway. The posts were seen as a form of public service and members were not paid. In the early 1980s that carefully thought through system was destroyed. In 1996, some 50,000 posts are in the Government's gift. Who actually makes these appointments? The Secretaries of State, according to their departmental briefs. All in the health sector, for example, are appointed by the Secretary of State for Health. The local MP is asked to comment, but generally at just a few hours' notice and in the voting lobby by the minister's Parliamentary Private Secretary.

Today there are, perhaps, two-thirds as many ministerial appointees in positions of local power in areas such as health as there are local councillors. The invisible hand of party political power is strongest here. Positions such as chairman of a local health authority used to be filled by people whose party political colour was not a weighting factor in their appointment. The overall political balance of a board might be adjusted at the end of the chain of new appointments by the injection of a balancing party member if a single other board member was known to be a local party member on top of his proffered expertise. Now members of boards – and most particularly their chairmen – are appointed *after* their political colours have been vetted, and thereafter flaunt their Conservative colours without constraint. Posts such as these are awarded by Government as consolation prizes for political failure, or as a convenient slot for former national or European MPs; or as a reward for long service to the party or family favour.

In 1994 I put my name forward as unobtrusively as possible for the Devon Euro-constituency, as one of a long list of other possible Conservative candidates. It was disconcerting to enter the room for an initial interview and to find among the committee of interviewers the chairman of a local health authority. It made it tough subsequently to maintain a professional relationship on health matters for my constituents where I believed the health authority was at fault. Our relationship had inevitably changed.

Of course, centralization of appointments discounts, by definition, factors that really matter to local people. How could the minister know that the people at Torrington felt isolated because no one from there had ever been appointed to the health authority board by the minister and the relevant office was two hours' drive away? Certainly, the people of Halwill Junction knew that their world was not properly understood when the funding for the small Winsford hospital, £250,000 a year, was pinpointed as the perfect sum to be used to fill the health authority's budget gap caused by an overrun on building costs elsewhere. Why should they lose a loving haven for the sick and dying, where families could drop in and help the staff and patients? Did not that calm and serenity in face of death matter? It could not be recreated once lost. Given the way in which the statistics used to justify the imminent closure were kept undisclosed, and the way in which the decision had been taken without proper local consultation, I personally agreed with them. It took all of my wit and strength to interest *Newsnight*; but they came down to film the public meeting, which was attended by over two thousand people. Their reporters talked to the patients and myself and were instrumental in helping us win the day. The health authority could not sustain their arguments under real public scrutiny. The minister made his own lack of interest in the case perfectly clear, casually remarking that he was closing hospitals all the time.

The exercise of the duty of political leadership by the elected Government must be built on compassion and competence, if the public are to be cared for as well as challenged. An overriding policy of binding your supporters to you by putting them in positions of simultaneous power and dependence diminishes competence and shreds and discards compassion, tossing it along with the needy out of the virtuous circle. Playing this game, the last two Conservative Governments have created probably the most powerful executive in the democratic world. New ministry positions have been created, new non-ministerial assistant posts have been made to support these new ministries and a exclusion zone has been drawn around these people and all the others occupying positions in the Government's gift. The Government's so-called payroll vote has expanded in numbers with the inclusion of Parliamentary Private Secretaries and chairmen of select committees, and in scope with its unseen application even to formally unwhipped votes of conscience, the traditionally free votes on matters of life and death (euthanasia, abortion, capital punishment) and issues affecting the whole body politic (such as Lord Nolan's Report). In fact, even for these 'free' votes a formal whipping system exists for everyone on the Government's payroll. A note is slipped into the party weekly whip stating that such a vote on such a day, which is on the official party whipping list as a free vote, is a mandatory pro-Government vote for the Minister and PPSs. The Government's position is passed round by muttered order. Thus, while the fiction of a 'free' vote is maintained in public, in reality it is just another 'turn up and go' day through the Government lobby. Hence the overtly bizarre statement of a minister recently when, urging the House to allow a debate, he promised a 'genuine free vote'. If it was genuine, it was the first from the Government's side for a very long time. By the 1992 general election the job of PPS was both an inducement to promotion and a constraint to follow the Government line in every possible respect.

A report in 1941 by the Select Committee on Offices for Profit noted both that a check in the number of ministers would be a good idea and, more specifically, that no ministerial department should have more than one Parliamentary Private Secretary. The Committee noted that the 'PPS, as he has come to be called, is a modern institution' whose 'independence as a Member of the House must be liable to be impaired to a somewhat greater extent than that of an ordinary Member of the Party supporting the Government in office'. This 'is, not without reason, regarded as increasing the voting strength and influence of the Government in the House of Commons'. Indeed, the 1992 Cabinet Office document *Questions of Procedure for Ministers* states that PPSs 'are expected to support the Government in all important divisions'. In 1900 there were nine PPSs in the House of Commons; by 1996 there were about fifty-six, including new posts created to serve the Conservative Party Chairman and the Leader of the House of Lords. As usual, on this matter the Government has sought to withhold relevant information from parliamentarians, as when Lord Wakeham, in a written answer of 4 November 1992, told Lord Rippon that information about the number of Parliamentary Private Secretaries in 1962 and 1972 was not held centrally. The appointment system used to be entirely in the hands of ministers, but certainly by 1992 the Whips' Office had taken over most of that function, creating a list of acceptable potential PPSs from which the minister had to choose. This gave the Whips an additional form of patronage, which was the main point as far as they were concerned; as far as the post of PPS itself went, one Whip dismissively described it as of less importance than the minister's driver.

The drawing of a sterilizing boundary between the Government's known loyalists and other, less reliable Conservative Members of Parliament was subtly encouraged. A Government loyalist would sit at a tea table. Comments not fully and instantly supportive of the Government's position would be reported back. Shortly afterwards a Whip would stop and reprimand the errant Member, quoting the precise words used earlier to a Conservative colleague. As the barriers against any divergent opinion have risen higher and higher, the number of Conservative backbenchers who share thoughts across them has shrunk, and independent thinkers such as Sir Richard Body attract vicious and public criticism, even from the Despatch Box.

The older Conservative Party had been very different, as had the relationship between the three national parties, one of political disagreement and largely personal goodwill. When, some time after he had left Parliament, my father became chairman of a board which had responsibility for mental health and psychiatric hospitals throughout Berkshire, Buckinghamshire and Oxfordshire, he did so at the personal request of Richard Crossman, Labour minister of health, and saw it as a public duty, not as a political appointment. By the time I left the Conservative Party, sharing a cup of coffee or tea with a non-Conservative was an offence, and even talking to a Conservative of a different political flavour a misdemeanour.

Questions of Procedure for Ministers also states that PPSs 'are not precluded from serving on Select Committees'; however, such participation was forbidden to me when I accepted the job of PPS, and I was forced to withdraw from the Select Committee on Employment, on which I had sat for two years. During that time I instigated investigations into employment of the disabled and employment in prisons. I tried to persuade the committee to accept new proposals from Europe on the protection of children at work. Real gains could be expected in child welfare in Greece and Portugal, for example, if such regulations were introduced and enforced. My argument hit a brick wall of prejudice.

There was a call for a member of the committee to volunteer to attend a meeting on European social policy in Brussels. I asked for briefing about the meeting, and particularly the Social Chapter, before I left. I was told there were no papers. No one knew what the meeting was about. When I arrived, I found the meeting had been planned a year before. This was the opportunity which was offered to national parliaments to be directly involved in the process of revising this part of the treaty. This meeting was the last round. Parliamentary delegations had come from every other member state, all bearing statements from their respective parliaments on amendments to the Social Chapter of the treaty at the IGC which was then in process. I was the only Briton. I had no papers. No statement. Nothing that I could say on my Parliament's behalf. Whatever ministers may say in public, it was clear that my own Government had no interest either in the substance of the social policy agenda or in MPs having a more direct role in European decisions.

An elderly man approached me, saying he was a clerk from the House of Lords attending in his own time. He could not remember when he had last seen a British MP at such a meeting; it was absolutely wonderful, he said, that I was there. I asked why no one came. 'The Government does not care,' he replied. 'They don't listen.'

As a former employer, I knew that the Social Chapter did not represent a very large advance on the position already reached in both European and British law. The biggest innovation was probably the introduction of majority voting into decisions affecting 'working conditions'. As far as legislation which has actually been passed under the Social Chapter is concerned, I can see nothing in it which lies outside the existing practice of good employers, though Britain's self-imposed absence from the negotiations has produced a more prescriptive approach than UK employers might like. The British Government has no real knowledge of what effect this legislation would have because it has not bothered to get involved. In any case, many of the complaints the Government directs at Brussels should more properly be directed at themselves, as became abundantly clear to me when I was a PPS in the Ministry of Agriculture, Fisheries and Food. Many of the regulations the farmers and fishermen complain about so much come not from Brussels but from the ministries and from the ministers themselves.

There was endless room for discussion and manoeuvre at that meeting in Brussels, even at that late stage in the consultation process. The Government could readily have picked out those elements which might have produced real difficulties in Britain. Problem areas could have been tackled over a longer time-scale while the major part went through. I felt utter despair. The Government was not dealing with the merits of the case. They talked about British employers and British jobs, but the real problem, from their point of view, was nothing to do with the world of work. The real problem lay within the Conservative Party itself.

In the end I did make a speech. I was lucky that the United Kingdom came last on the speaker's list alphabetically, giving me time to prepare. Everybody said how astonishing it was to find a British Member of Parliament there at all. Afterwards I went to find some of the Conservative Members of the European Parliament and asked what was going on. Echoing the words of the clerk to whom I had spoken earlier, they said: 'People don't bother. The Government does not care. And we are isolated from the British Government on this and from the Conservative Party even though we are British MEPs. It is just appalling.' That is the truth. No wonder we fail in Europe. We don't bother to turn up.

*

Between 1990 and 1993 I was repeatedly warned by those close to John Major that my name was 'in the frame' and that he wanted me to be a minister. Each time, as warned, I readied myself to decide what to do, and each time I was not, after all, contacted. Subsequently, I was told several times that John Major was very sorry he couldn't give me any responsibility because I was so unpopular with some of the parliamentary wives. I found the whole thing incomprehensible and tried from time to time to find out what lay behind this sequence of suggestions and their withdrawal. None of it fitted; I didn't understand why I should continually be warned if nothing would ever happen. It was ironic that I should be deemed unpopular with women, given how hard I had worked to promote their role in the party while I had been a volunteer in Central Office.

Prior to each reshuffle in this period, therefore, I was bothered by the idea of promotion. For a long time I believed that if there was a chance of reaching a position of real influence from which I could change things for the better, I should take it. I did not relish the climate of intense competition for promotion; but whatever my criticisms, I continued to accept that the only effective course for a Conservative was to pursue change from within. In 1990, just after he had failed to win the leadership contest, I asked Michael Heseltine if he would allow me to serve as his PPS. He refused very brusquely; I never asked again. In 1992, however, after the June election, I was appointed as a Parliamentary Private Secretary. This put paid to my speaking out on issues which were considered inconvenient for the Government; but I accepted the gag, believing that, if I progressed further inside the political charmed circle, I would be able to influence ministerial views for the better. My optimism proved ill-founded. The twin cultures of party secrecy and ministerial self-seeking had overwhelmed the efforts of those who, like Earl Ferrers, Ken Clarke and Lord Mackay, sought the common good.

Later on, I was brought up short by the comment of a distinguished and respected colleague, one of the most obviously wasted Conservative intellects of his generation. We were talking one day when he turned to me and said, 'You know, Emma, the difference between you and me is that you would take a job from this rotten Government. I wouldn't touch one.' I reflected for a second. He was right. I thought through my whole position and started to disentangle myself from the system. I could do more good from the back benches, certainly for my constituents. I hung on for one more year as a PPS, however, until my minister left MAFF, since local farmers liked me to be close to the department and to try to influence its policies. It proved to be the least productive year of my long working life.

Chapter 10

More Questions than Answers

We won the election in Devon West and Torridge in 1992 thanks to my voting Mrs Thatcher out of power, combined with the consistent and high-quality constituency work that Ruth Manning, my constituency secretary, and I had carried out so diligently and for so long. Countless people came out of their houses to tell me that they didn't usually vote Conservative but that they would this time. I had got rid of the poll tax for them by voting against Mrs Thatcher and they had not forgotten. Or they referred to a letter I had written which had broken the log-jam of bureaucracy and given them fair treatment. One mother came out to say that her whole family would support me. Three years ago I had learned of her young son's terminal cancer and his campaign to buy a computer for his local school from the local newspaper, the *North Devon Journal*, a weekly packed with local information and barely a smidgeon of politics. I had given a private donation. Her son had gone into remission, and now she wanted to show her gratitude. As I had found in Blyth and throughout the UK, people's sincerity, their honesty, their sense of political right and wrong, struck me anew as the one underlying certainty in British democracy.

I fought my campaign with a skeleton voluntary team headed by our association president, an elderly, unwell farmer, gasping up and down the Devon hills in an antiquated and battered bus which I had hired. I had been forced into this by the refusal of some key local party workers who had supported Mrs Thatcher to campaign for me, and the support of the chairman, Geoffrey Cleverdon, was very patchy. Could his absence from the field of battle at the critical eve-of-poll stage in 1992 have been linked to his belief that we would lose the day?

Many other Conservative canvassers declined to come out in 1992, but for most of them this was because they felt in an impossible situation. Working for the Conservatives on the doorstep meant having to argue for the Conservative record, in spite of clear evidence that family, friends and neighbours had suffered as a result of Government actions. Indeed, as other members of the South West group of Conservative MPs said to me so frequently, what had John Major or Margaret Thatcher before him done for the south-west? Unless you incorporated Bristol in the statistics (a handy ploy of which Government statements made full use), all that could be perceived was a relative decline in many of the things that counted – especially if, as so many of our constituents did, you lived in a farming village with one bus service a week to a distant town. People trusted the professional services and those who delivered them, the doctors, the teachers, the vicars and ministers, and realized from daily life that even the professionals' complaints were as real as their own. Local people and local leaders found common ground in their dissatisfaction with the Government's record.

By 1996 water bills in the south-west were 62 per cent above the national average and the highest throughout England and Wales. There was little regional assistance; European funding allocated to the south-west for 1994–9 was held back by the Treasury, and after two years only £6 million had reached projects on the ground. The imbalance between the regions had become more marked: the annual grant to Scotland for tourism and development had reached £16.9 million while that to the south-west was a mere £0.4 million – despite the fact that the tourist industry is the source of 23 per cent of Cornwall's GDP. A 1995 report by accountants Coopers & Lybrand stated that, overall, Devon and Cornwall received under £50 million a year in Government aid, compared with £187 million a year for Wales and £530 million for Scotland. And yet the south-west is the region of the UK with the lowest average household income, running at 20 per cent below the national average.

South-west MPs tried to explain regional problems, particularly water bills, to the Prime Minister. Occasional meetings were held in his House of Commons office, over tea and biscuits around a long polished mahogany table. The excitement beforehand was palpable. Everyone felt that his or her point would be the one that would be heard. The team would assemble, faces betraying eagerness, notes ready for memory refreshment – too many of us for discussion, too few for an audience for a speech. The tension would then ebb as John Major prolonged his earlier discussions, or was just late. He did not give the impression of really wishing to see us; he would read an official-looking note, add his 'be friends with me, I need you' smile and ask for points, saying always that he was late. Peter Emery or Anthony Steen would rush people through their rehearsed statements, grouped for maximum effect. The discussion would turn swiftly to how to react to media requests for the results of the meeting. As there were never any results this should not have been a problem. However, earnest pledges were sought and obtained that the meeting should be in confidence lest some wonderful unspoken future potential result be jeopardized by a chance disclosure. This discussion successfully took up the remaining meeting time. Nothing had been agreed. The MPs left, verbose with gratitude, and five minutes later several of them would be stopping in the Members' Lobby and earnestly briefing the local newspapers and radio stations. Afterwards they would apologize to the others: somehow they'd got waylaid.

Back in the Chamber again with fresh expression of my constituents' experiences reinforcing my own perception, I saw that the British people were not getting the Government that they deserved and wanted. The deficiencies of the party in power were acutely noted by Ryszard Herczynski, an internationally eminent mathematician who came to Britain as a member of the Cultural Department of the Polish Embassy in

London. He observed the stagnation, the lack of any sense of purpose or direction: 'The current problems (difficult as they are) dominate long-term considerations; . . . pragmatism became more and more opportunistic: the realistic, reasonable approach by Government is not (and should not be) the same as that of conformism. Nor should there be any retreat from matters of principle because of the particular interests of the day.'

Competence, to me, is something more than the mere exercise of power. That, after all, within the five-year electoral cycle, is the easy part. Once you have taken control, once your party 'are the rulers now', it's just a question of getting the work done. In a democracy, to exercise power when elected is one thing; to remain in power over a long period is trickier. But this the Conservative Party has managed for two-thirds of the present century. Of course, this string of victories is in large part a quirk of the first-past-the-post system: successive Conservative Party Governments, at least since the Second World War, have been elected by a minority vote. In 1992 Neil Kinnock and the Labour Party polled 43 per cent of the vote but took only 42 per cent of the seats, whereas the Conservative Party, with 42 per cent of the vote, took 52 per cent of the seats. But leaving aside the unfairness of the present electoral system, what are the practicalities of staying in power? The first imperative is to keep pleasing those who matter in your search to sustain your own or your party's position. In practice, this means you have to trade power for support by giving your backers a significant slice of the action. Thus, if your priority is to stay in power, you cannot be free to give power to those who might use it to best effect for the wider good. The greater good has to be subordinated to the overriding task of keeping your own supporters happy.

It was after the 1992 election that I was invited by Michael Jack to be his Parliamentary Private Secretary in the Home Office. This was a man whose thoroughness and consistency of work, as well as his cheerful outlook, I knew and liked. For a year thereafter I had the pleasure of working in a team led by Kenneth Clarke and including Earl Ferrers, Peter Lloyd, a top-rate person of the highest standards, and the elegant and quick-witted Tessa Keswick, now head of the Centre for Policy Studies and then Kenneth Clarke's political adviser. His PPS at this time was the saturnine Philip Oppenheim, who later moved on to become a minister, the goal of nearly every PPS.

There was, of course, a price to be paid for this inclusion in the official circle: although I had no real influence and no responsibility, I was instructed to behave like a member of the Government, never publicly questioning any aspect of Government policy, let alone voting against it. My own small duties as a PPS also put an end for the time being to my work on computer pornography, computer crime, freedom of information and data protection. I had to step down from anything even remotely connected with the Home Office, including the Howard League for Penal Reform and a number of other organizations. I resigned as founder Chairman of the European Information Market All-Party Group just as we were making real headway in Brussels. I was sorry that my parliamentary successors commercialized it by creating a company.

While the post of PPS was still unpaid, a condition of entry was a Trappist vow of silence, for which the limited reward was participation in – or, at least, attendance at – the regular departmental ministerial meetings, known disrespectfully as 'Prayers'. There was a strict order of precedence at Prayers, even in the seating plan, which was in some cases drawn up by the ministers. There was always a Whip on duty, and sometimes the minister's private secretary, who was privy to nearly everything, was also present. The substance, content and tone of these meetings, as well as their usefulness, varied according to the Secretary of State in charge. In 1992 with Kenneth Clarke in the lead, Home Office meetings took place over a sandwich lunch and were boisterous and challenging. Kenneth accepted ideas and comments from every corner of the room, regardless of the speaker's status. At the Ministry of Agriculture under

Gillian Shephard, Prayers were held at nine in the morning and the atmosphere was very party political. Mrs Shephard was aided at first by Julian Brazier, her long-serving PPS, and by her political adviser, Dr Elizabeth Cottrell. Elizabeth should have been a minister herself, but more than once was defeated by the Conservative Party's aversion to women candidates. Gillian Shephard was succeeded at the agriculture ministry by William Waldegrave, and the intellectual tone of the meetings rose. I took the opportunity of the change at the top to raise for the second time an evasion of the rules on the export of cattle that was worrying me immensely. I had been deeply concerned to discover a well-orchestrated scheme among certain farmers who were forging forms to enable them to export cattle as from BSE-free herds when they were not, thus risking the spread of the infection. William reacted swiftly and put his staff on the case. The consequence was a series of prosecutions which have already cost some fraudulent farmers dear.

As a PPS I became an expert at dishing out parliamentary questions, and in the process became deeply troubled about the manipulation of parliamentary business. The matter of parliamentary questions may seem esoteric or irrelevant, but in fact they are one of the most important means by which the Executive is held to account for its actions. A good PPS can reduce this mechanism to a public conversation which the minister holds with himself for the benefit of the Government.

Each minister answered parliamentary questions once every four weeks. The questions were put together by the political adviser, on the instruction of the minister and in liaison with the desk officer at Conservative Central Office. Having been approved by the ministers, the questions were then handed out to the Parliamentary Private Secretaries for distribution to MPs. We stood in the Members' Lobby with batches of questions, pre-typed, pre-addressed to the minister, pre-dated and with the date of answer. Our job was to get Conservative Members of Parliament to accept and table these questions. I became very good at this; people were very kind in taking questions from me. The questions went into a shuffle; every evening a dip was made by the clerks on duty and as the questions came out they were labelled in order and became the list of 'oral questions'. In a good week, I and my fellow PPSs from our department would get down sixty or seventy such 'planted' questions. This meant there was a good chance that a substantial proportion of the questions that day would have come from the ministers themselves. The Conservative Party Whip for the department – there was one for each department – would keep a list of the strike-rate and tick them off, so there was a form of competition among the Parliamentary Private Secretaries as to who had got the most planted questions selected in the shuffle. We managed up to 60 per cent of all the oral questions.

The following week, the CCO desk officer and the minister's political adviser would hold a meeting with all the PPSs to create the supplementary questions. A week later, on the day for parliamentary questions, the PPSs were given batches of printed supplementaries to hand out among the attending backbenchers. The ministers already had the answers to both the planted questions and the planted supplementary questions. One day I achieved the perfect record for a PPS: I managed to get a planted answer to a planted supplementary to a planted answer to a planted question. The whole thing had come from the minister, who had originally created the question. For this farcical achievement I was heartily congratulated by the Whips.

Ministers and Whips then thought up a further refinement, setting up formal, pre-Question Time meetings to brief the questioners, to groom them in advance so that, once in the Chamber, they would bob up and down obediently, mouthing pre-formulated inanities. These meetings were organized and held by the Parliamentary Private Secretaries half an hour before Question Time, in the large ministerial conference room. The Secretary of State, or senior minister, sat in the chair, flanked by more junior ministers and beyond them, to left and right, the PPSs. Any junior minister who failed to appear earned an unofficial black mark. Batches of supplementary question papers were distributed as the Members came in, summoned by letter or telephone call. Some glinted with ambition, endlessly bright-eyed, constantly searching for assurances of their worth. Others were the intelligent endurers, on the way out at the next election. Lastly came those who had once been the young idealists, now more realistic and despairing of ever making any impact on the Executive. For the next half an hour the Secretary of State and the ministers took this audience of twenty or thirty backbenchers through the questions and answers, and the supplementary questions and the supplementary answers, until everyone was clear precisely what performance was to be put on that afternoon and was word-perfect in his or her part as a member of the chorus. At twenty-five past the hour, under starter's orders, a few MPs would race out to claim their named and reserved places in the Chamber, to be ready for the off.

The Conservative Party has a ritual peculiar to itself in the reservation of seats in the Commons Chamber. Liberal Democrat and Labour Members just come in and sit down. Some Conservative Members, however, come in during the morning with cards inscribed with their names, which they put in certain seats, thus reserving them for their personal use for the remainder of the day. I once fell foul of this system when attempting to make best use of it. I had spotted a free seat that would be especially useful to me in hearing as well as possible. It was usually occupied by a portly and very senior Member, but on this occasion was unexpectedly vacant. Perhaps he was away. I put my name on it. When I came back in later there he was, bellowing with rage that 'his' seat had been taken. In vain did I point out that he had not put a green card on it. His friends nearby turned on me. He should have it, they said; they always took the same seats themselves. He tossed away my card. To him, the possession of a prime position seemed to mean almost more than life itself. I crawled away.

At 2.30 p.m. Madam Speaker took the Chair and those in the ministerial team who had not gone into prayers lined up outside the Chamber. As soon as prayers were over, the doors opened and in they strode: the ministers on the front bench, carrying their dignity with them, the PPSs behind them with an eye to the civil servants' box where bits of paper carrying urgent data might be waved for speedy collection and urgent transmission to the minister. The drilled backbenchers, briefed and hopeful, brimful with knowledge, satisfied that their spot would be covered at least by local television, settled back expectantly in their seats, named or otherwise. The Speaker called the name of the first Member listed, who stood up and dutifully intoned: 'Question number one, Madam Speaker.' The afternoon's charade had begun. But the age-old practice of democracy by Members examining and challenging the Executive had gone.

*

In 1993 the first piece of legislation under the Maastricht Treaty came through. I made a speech in the Commons saying that the most important thing we could do in the European Union was to look very carefully at the impact of European legislation on the domestic legal framework. If European institutions were to exercise their powers by consent, it was important that national interests were protected. I knew that Brussels was not just harmonizing, but initiating legislation, which made this of increasing importance. I still found it difficult to believe that some ministers did not fully understand the way in which European legislation worked or that we had voluntarily agreed to all the treaty obligations. I was astonished that Britain's long membership of the EU had resulted in such a grave and deep misunderstanding. Such was the penalty, I felt, for not playing a full part in this Club of Clubs, in leaving the chair empty in so many important meetings. It meant that the substance of what was going on was lost to us.

During the debate on the Maastricht Treaty the Conservative Party's continued refusal to brief either its supporters or the wider electorate properly over European issues had become ever clearer to me. I spent considerable amounts of time during this period responding to invitations to speak to constituences to explain the treaty and the new obligations that it would confer if Parliament were to pass it. I found that the constituency Conservative associations lacked even basic knowledge of the subject. Indeed, I could not find a single Conservative activist who had even read the Treaty of Rome, let alone the Single European Act. The likelihood that they would have looked at the detail of Maastricht was, therefore, nil. All the material was readily available directly from Brussels; surely it should also be obtainable from Smith Square? I contacted the Conservative Research Department. Was there a small amount of literature on the Maastricht Treaty that I could distribute to local members? I asked. The reply was that this was the preserve of the European constituency associations; any material on Europe went directly to them – though actually there wasn't much on Maastricht, only a leaflet or two that had been put together just recently.

But the people I was addressing in the constituencies were begging for knowledge. I went to the Party Chairman, Norman Fowler, and suggested that, as a one-off gesture, Central Office arrange for material to be sent directly to the constituency associations, not the European Conservative Councils (the party bodies who nursed the EP seats). When he declined, I did some more tours myself, taking cases full of material which my audiences pounced on. Central Office was reluctant to send speakers round the constituency associations to explain the facts and leave them literature to read. Once again, the Conservative Party deliberately left its supporters in ignorance, about a matter it was supporting up and down the land, all over the newspapers, on the television and through the radio. The leadership was perfectly prepared to leave local party activists without the essential knowledge they needed, first to make up their own minds on the merits of the case and secondly to persuade their members and the outside world of the Government's own views.

Through my own work, I had generated a greater flow of British expertise into the European legislative process, particularly on copyright, patents and design and on computer software and crime. I suggested to the European legislators new ways of examining their own proposals and different groups of experts that might be consulted. I found the European Union very open to constructive suggestions of this nature, and within weeks new groups were set up including significant numbers of British experts. Working with ECHO, the European Community humanitarian aid organization, which later consistently co-financed my work in the AMAR Appeal for the southern Iraqi victims of Saddam Hussein, brought me into contact with some of the finest minds I know. Like most highly committed, intelligent people, they welcomed new thoughts. Britain, by contrast, seemed to me to be operating in a way where excellence and innovative thought came way down the list, where clinging to old concepts for their own sake alone was seen as a strength and not as a weakness. Many Conservative MPs, indeed, seemed to take great pride in ignoring what was going on a stone's throw away across the Channel. Anthony Lewis, writing in the *New York Times* of 11 June 1996, wondered whether such insularity would ever be overcome: 'A delusion underlies the continuing reluctance [of Britain] to embrace the European idea: the delusion that, at the end of the twentieth century, in a world market, a country the size of Britain can have total sovereignty. France and Germany, equally proud in their history, got the point long ago. Whether Britain ever will remains uncertain.'

Chapter 11

A Sick System

The sale of South West Water gave privatization a bad name in the West Country. Although I had argued, logically, at the time that the people of London could not be expected to pay for cleaning up the beach at Croyde, I had no doubt at all that water bills had risen to levels which were intolerable for large sections of the community. What privatization did for water bills, the uniform business rate did for sub-post offices. Though it had appeared sound in principle, a valid means of protecting small businesses from the profligacy of extreme left-wing councils, the uniform business rate actually resulted in the death by strangulation of many small post offices. It was five years before a Conservative Manifesto Working Party in MAFF concluded that sub-post offices should have a fairer deal because they were serving isolated communities and were suffering a catastrophic loss of profitability.

It was against that background, as I said to Michael Heseltine early in 1995, that it would not be possible for me to support post office privatization. As a general rule, Michael Heseltine makes no secret of his own importance. On this occasion, he made no secret of his annoyance either. From the full height of his exalted office as President of the Board of Trade (surely a post and maybe a ministry to abolish) he peered down at my puny form and told me that was the 'last straw'; he wouldn't go ahead.

Time and again the remnants of public confidence in the Government have been undermined by its wilful refusal to confront realities, combined with a damaging inconsistency.

Take health care and the example of small local hospitals. For years the Government took a negative line; health care was best met by large hospitals with everything on offer under one roof. The personal wishes of patients and their relatives that people should be treated close to home were dismissed. Then, after many hospitals had been closed, the Secretary of State announced that community hospitals offered the best provision of health for the future.

An even more culpable failure of Government in respect of public health occurred in the face of the threat posed by BSE and CJD. The Southwood Committee studied the emergence of BSE and came up with very sensible and soundly based recommendations. The Government accepted them and issued instructions that they should be followed, but put no enforcement measures in place. Moreover, ministers made statements that were unsupported by the research evidence of the Southwood Committee. Unwarrantable commercial constraints were put on research. The interdepartmental group studying the neuro-degenerative diseases came to be dominated by MAFF. This baulked any research that might have harmed the close relations between MAFF and food producers. Research briefs have even set out the answers desired before the work is done. I heard MAFF ministers fighting fiercely to retain their hold on public health matters related to food consumption, to the exclusion of the Ministry of Health. The result of all these machinations has been to let down consumers and farmers alike.

Health ministers had their own code of secrecy and control over knowledge. I argued strenuously with a minister and his civil servants for the release of stored patient data to that small group of youngsters who, unknown to themselves or their families, might well be incubating CJD derived from a human source, infected cadaver pituitary glands, which had been used to assist their childhood growth. I believed strongly that, once this information was in the hands of the ministry (as it had been for some years), the young men and women affected should also know. Eventually, after considerable and sustained effort, the minister agreed, reluctantly, only to alert the families' GPs.

In the autumn of 1994 I challenged my own Conservative Party local members and, in a way, myself, saying that we

> must get away from the idea of what Conservatism stands for that has now emerged. It is not just about money, or opposing change; Conservatism is not a hard-faced, ego-centred doctrinal creed. It is a generous spirit of tolerance towards others, which sets firm boundaries of personal behaviour based on sound principles of respect for everyone and for the traditions we've inherited. Our task is to sustain and hand on the best of British political values to our successors.

At that October's party conference, I knew that I was wrong. A new and very different Conservatism had emerged. For calling on old-style, one-nation values to justify my arguments on social justice at a packed fringe debate I was jeered at and cat-called as a 'semi-detached' Conservative. My very presence as a panel-list on a fringe meeting on housing was rudely challenged by a junior minister, who afterwards told the Whips I'd spoken against him: I was reprimanded, although several senior party officials in the audience were unable to see why. Even an expression of a minor variance from the Government line – one which, in the event, was later incorporated into Government policy – could not, it seemed, be tolerated.

Even the previous year, at the 1993 conference, I had seen that Conservatism was no longer all the things I had believed it was, and still wanted it to be. I was dismayed by the attacks from the platform made by John Redwood and John Major on highly vulnerable women, in the name of a specious appeal to get 'back to basics'. This campaign was a particularly cynical sham which unravelled with exceptional speed. Within three months it

had tripped up on the revelation that Tim Yeo MP had fathered
an illegitimate child; this news was followed a month later by the
tragic death of Stephen Milligan MP. I had spoken against John
Redwood immediately, while still at the conference, at another
fringe meeting, saying that the nature of family life had altered.
On 8 February 1994 I spoke out against the misguided
campaign on the BBC, saying: 'I think it's time we let this "back
to basics" slogan drop. It's got too many sad connotations for us
as a party. I hope that we can forget it.' Within hours I was
being bawled out. Who was I talking to? He was the First Lord
of the Treasury and the Government Chief Whip. Who did I
think I was? Daring to comment on Government policy when
my job, and my only job, was to support all Government policy
all the time, even if I'd never heard of it or disagreed with it? I
was forbidden to disagree with the Prime Minister, and
forbidden to do any more broadcasts or speak to the press on
anything for the following six weeks, or to make speeches.

The voice was that of Richard Ryder, but to me the words,
and the anger behind them, came from John Major. I left the
bubble of fury and went straight out to do a radio broadcast.

I was by no means the only unhappy member of the Tory
Party, either then or afterwards. But my words seemed to touch
a particularly raw nerve with the party managers. I never
discovered why. The 'back to basics' campaign was continued
for only a few more days; the Government's abuse of power in
this highly insensitive attack on the recipients of Parliament-
approved financial benefits for one of the poorest groups in
society proved insupportable to many. The following week the
campaign died. I could only hope my intervention had helped it
on its way.

I was particularly sorry to see the intense strain to which this
ill-advised and misdirected campaign had subjected backbenchers who were vulnerable in their private lives as they
struggled to keep untypical relationships away from the Whips'
scrutiny, or to find a Conservative-style partner. In fact it was

the Conservative parliamentary party itself that lay at the heart of the sleaze that surrounded the Commons – as became only too apparent when the national press came alive to standards of behaviour in the Palace of Westminster.

I was glad to see the Nolan Committee set up in October 1994. In an ideal world, a Parliament which regulates the nation should be able to regulate itself. However, the behaviour of too many MPs and peers had made it abundantly clear that the assumptions of gentlemanly behaviour and personal honour upon which the system of self-regulation relied for its success were no longer enough. The wider decline in the effectiveness of the House of Commons that had accompanied the decline in standards of public conduct was pinpointed by Liberal Democrat Robert Maclennan in the debate of 6 November 1995:

> This is not entirely a debate about political morality. It is also – and should be – a debate about the effectiveness of this House. It is not just the venal behaviour . . . of – I believe – not very many Members of Parliament that should be under the spotlight. It is also the inadequacy of Parliament to discharge the functions required of it that has fostered the growth of lobbying which in turn has led to the problems that we face today.

I gave evidence to Lord Nolan's Committee in January 1995. Aware of the need to limit any damage which my evidence might do to my own party, I trod as carefully as I could. This did not prevent my being intercepted by a Whip within half an hour of leaving the committee room to be told that I had been acting against other colleagues and betraying the party. Perhaps that explains why so few Conservatives gave evidence – despite the Prime Minister's public exhortation when setting up the Nolan Committee in October 1994, 'Naturally, I would expect Ministers and Members of Parliament to give evidence to the Committee if requested to do so . . .'

On its publication in May 1995, the Prime Minister welcomed both the spirit and the substance of the Nolan Report. No matter how inventive the party's draughtsmen may be with the English language, the gap between the Prime Minister's statements, made in public, and the strictures of the Whips, pressed in private, was unbridgeable. Then the Prime Minister announced the establishment of a committee to examine Lord Nolan's findings, and my heart sank. I wanted to vote against it. I was told by the Whips that there was no need; the issue of substance would be the final vote on the committee's report. So I obediently voted in favour. I have had many letters over the years from victims of doubtful enterprises of all kinds. I know exactly how they feel. I watched the committee's work and I realized that it had been nobbled. The Prime Minister's declaration in favour of the spirit of Nolan looked honourable when it was uttered; it looked far from honourable by the time the 'issue of substance' was finally put before the House.

It was clear to me now that my time as a PPS was coming to an end. Even before the first report of the Select Committee on Standards in Public Life came out, I knew that it was not likely that I would be able to support it. Also, the Scott Report would be coming out before long, and I knew too much about the supply of arms to Iraq and the extent to which Parliament had been misled to be able to back the Government on that either. I knew from the Iraqi side that a British company had supplied arms to Iraq as well as material for making biological and chemical weapons. Further, the Prime Minister's dissociation of himself from the pattern of events that had unfolded during his time in the Treasury, the Foreign Office and Number Ten meant that the buck stopped nowhere. To me, ignorance was no defence, and his submission in evidence, in which he said that he did not know what was going on, demonstrated clearly to me that he should have held none of these jobs. Such positions should have been held by someone who would have taken the trouble to find out and grasp the information flowing through his ministry in relation to the world's most dangerous tyrant, heading the cruellest regime since Hitler's. It would not be possible for me to support the Government on the Scott Report.

Also, that summer, the asylum legislation was having its inevitable effect on my postbag. The legislation of the previous year, which I had unwillingly supported, had proved to be a licence to bully the weak, the helpless, the inarticulate, the sick, the dumb. Horrifying tales were coming to me of people denied the most basic human rights, such as to visit a family member in England when they were dying. This was not the fault of the civil servants; the rules were viciously exclusive. As if this were not enough, a new Bill was on its way to take away the right to bed and breakfast provision of mothers and children, babies and grandmothers, who had somehow got into Britain and were waiting for their cases to be heard. I could not support this. Nor did I think I would be called on to speak in the House, given the combination of the constraints on a PPS to support the Government and my prolonged inability to catch Madam Speaker's eye; or, with my views, get on to the Asylum Bill Standing Committee.

I realized that the best thing I could do was to resign my post as a PPS at once. I had long since realized that it was the role of a stooge, designed to keep people quiet without giving them a means of changing things for the better. I was occupying a political no-man's land, peopled only by the mute figures of the other PPSs. Sitting there in silence, unable to fight their corner, I was letting my constituents down; moreover, by holding office I was, in however small a way, validating the system as a whole.

But I did not want to cause my minister inconvenience or embarrassment; even though I found myself ever more frequently opposed to the Government's measures, I liked and respected a number of colleagues whose views were similar to mine and tried to get them promotion. I also believed that the Prime Minister himself dealt fairly with all comers and had the good of the country at heart. However, by July 1995, my respect for him had evaporated. By this stage, it seemed to me, his priority was to survive at any cost, and for no one's sake other than his own. It was time for me to leave the backwaters of Government. Clearly the best moment to go was in the recess, but before the party conference; that way, no one would notice.

Through the summer I started to think hard about the Asylum Bill. It would be large and complicated; to oppose it effectively, I would have to take many briefings from outside organizations such as the Refugee Council. I talked to the office of the UNHCR. Despite their natural desire to work effectively with Home Office ministers, their view was as uncompromising as my own. It was perhaps indicative of the Government's approach that the Home Secretary, Michael Howard, was so unwilling to meet with Philippe Lavanchy, the UNHCR's Commissioner in Britain. I worked with Philippe throughout the summer on a particular and difficult case in which I had been involved since 1991; he was unstinting in his responses to my calls for help. The Foreign Office, as usual, exercised its knowledge and skills to fully professional effect; in an international matter of this kind, I saw these officials as my benchmark of quality. The Home Office officials, on the other hand, diligent, delightful and assiduous though they were, were hamstrung by the Home Secretary's determination to have no knowledge of the human condition. Struggling with Michael Howard was a nightmare.

In accordance with the decision I had reached in the summer, early in September I wrote a regretful note to the minister whose cause I had served for three years and through three ministries. I genuinely wished him well. He was an honest broker. By the middle of the month I realized that I could not honourably take the party conference in my stride. I stayed away as Michael Portillo laid into Brussels.

For the last two years it had been becoming clearer and clearer to me that the British people were fundamentally uneasy with what was going on. What they really wanted was real change: not just a change of personnel, or even a change of party, but a change in the way that our democracy functions, particularly within the House of Commons. The way to bring about such change is not to change the wallpaper from blue to red or the faces of the quango members from purple to pink. It is to change the way we make up the House of Commons so that the sensible people, the centre-ground people, are in the majority. Nor would they all be in one party; they could be of several parties, slightly left, slightly right, slightly centre. The only way towards this is through change in the voting system.

Imagine the impression of Britain which is given by the House of Commons, especially the Conservative benches. Anyone who inferred the nature of British society from those benches would be sadly misled. Much of the vibrancy and energy of Britain derives from its very diversity. We need a Parliament which reflects our cultural make-up, our ethnic mix, the gender balance and Britain's many different disciplines, professions and occupations. Instead, while Britain has become more varied, the Tory Party has become an ever narrower clique.

Today, and for some time, it has been an impossibility for a Conservative MP to have friends across the board. Any attempt to talk to somebody in a different wing of the party, or group within a wing, arouses hostility, resentment, nervousness that you may somehow be going to rock their boat or steal information for use by another group, or even betray them by reporting a comment back to a Whip and so bring disciplinary action down on their heads. It is a climate of fear; no divergence of opinion is allowed, and an unguarded comment will bring an immediate response, if not from a Whip then from some party busybody, with the swift dagger blow of 'I hear you've been criticizing Government policy,' or 'Am I right in thinking that someone heard you not supporting the Government line? You must be more careful what you say as I am sure you wouldn't want that impression to emerge even among colleagues.' The fear is tangible. Unspoken threats, promises of baubles and a constant rattling of the Whips' Office personal secrets folder (the infamous Black Book) have fragmented the Parliamentary Conservative Party and left it without either voice or vision for the future.

The modern Conservative Member of Parliament is someone who has picked up politics maybe at the age of ten or eleven. They don't know what they are talking about. They want to cling on to the coat-tails of those already in power and rise with them. They are drawn by the spurious glamour of right-wing power which seems so attractive to boys in their teens. They enjoy the certainty of ideology. They do not hesitate to carve up the society of which they know so little into sections, focusing their prejudices on first one segment, then another: single mothers one week, the unemployed the next. The old boy network of the traditional Conservative Party may have been difficult for women to break into; but it was held together by a sense of community. It was also a small community. This meant that if somebody felt that his point of view was very important, he would have a word with the minister and try to do something about it. Now there is no one listening: the Party seems to be operating in an atmosphere of fear and dislike of its own members. There is a lack of mutual respect in the Conservative Party which is bringing great unhappiness. Unprecedented numbers of MPs are leaving, and parliamentary careers are becoming shorter. People are voting with their feet.

Parliament badly needs reform. We need to examine all the possible ways of voting, of making up a House of Commons that will once again be close to the people and their needs. This can only be done by proportional representation of some description. Our 'first past the post' system triggers a shock wave reaction through the Westminster and Whitehall seats of power, starting with the post of Prime Minister and reverberating down to the humblest local benefice. Every position which can be said to have some political advantage, from the greatest to the lowliest, goes to the victor. He gains the entirety of the spoils of the election war – now more than ever, after so long a war of attrition by the Conservative Party against the largely unwritten inherited checks and balances. This breeds a culture of conceit which after a number of years subtly corrupts even the establishment of the Palace of Westminster too. Staff here start to connive with the Government in a way that is unfavourable to the Opposition and which diminishes the equal respect, if not equal agreement, between the ruler and the ruled which is the vital underpinning of Britain's democracy. This accretion of power to the centre has been extended under the Conservative Party in recent years to encompass areas formerly subject to decentralized power. Countless existing arrangements and provisions at both local and national level which formerly provided democratic checks and balances have been destroyed, either by direct assault, as under Mrs Thatcher, or by carelessness or lack of understanding.

If the resulting system gives the outsider an impression of one-party rule, that is not so far off the truth. A head of state such as South Africa's President Mandela comes to address both Houses of Parliament. Out of the whole panoply of elected figures who meet him, only the Speaker, and that by chance, is neither a Conservative Member nor a Tory Peer. The distinguished visitor is greeted and escorted by the Lord Chancellor, himself a member of the Conservative Cabinet; the Prime Minister, who is also the Party Leader; the Conservative Leader in the House of Lords, Lord Cranborne; and the Conservative Leader of the House of Commons, Tony Newton. Inside the Hall some Conservative Members, after the manner of package tourists on holiday in the Costa del Sol, send family members ahead with stacks of newspapers to claim and hold fast scores of seats in the front rows before they themselves deign to appear, up to an hour later.

After seventeen years much of the Opposition has got used to being treated as a doormat. The fear is lest the Labour Party, seeing themselves as an incoming Government, play the same tricks. Some are already, and for all the wrong reasons, showing signs of that air of conceit on the basis of little virtue exhibited by so many Conservatives now. Even the Civil Service has not been entirely immune to the centripetal forces. In all three of the ministries in which I worked, I saw that the Civil Service had been brought so close to party politics that lines were constantly being crossed over, even redrawn. Civil servants' job security was put at risk by ministers becoming ever more closely involved in appointments, with an inevitable political bias. Permanent Secretaries can now lose their jobs so that a ministerial favourite can be brought in. Ministers now feel free to criticize senior civil servants heavily, in their absence, for not taking up a particular political position; this happens frequently at the departmental political teams' morning 'Prayer Meetings'. In 1995, party polit-ical manifesto material and associated meetings were organized and assembled in ministry offices as a matter of course. No one queried this until *Private Eye* made a partial disclosure.

Civil servants struggled against this onslaught. It was to their credit that so many of them managed to maintain the degree of internal, professional, personal neutrality that they did. Perhaps Lord Armstrong, as Cabinet Secretary and Head of the Home Civil Service, inadvertently caused more damage than was recognized outside the Government when in his seminal 1985 note on *The Duties and Responsibilities of Civil Servants in Relation to Ministers* – possibly the first important document on the subject since the late Victorian reforms – he declared that the first loyalty of civil servants is to the Government of the day. This is surely wrong, since in our system a Government, once elected, even by a minority, now wields near-absolute power. The Armstrong paper begged the question of how the Civil Service should react if Government were to take the sort of extreme line that several ministers have done latterly. Surely the Civil

Service should be responsible to democracy? Who now stands up for the citizen? Even once staunch Conservatives are starting to express concern, although they phrase it somewhat differently from the way I did, even while still in the party. In their view everything is 'all right' under the Conservatives; but they are worried that once another party takes power it could control Britain's entire universe. I believe that recent developments strengthen the case for a written constitution.

The central reform that is needed, head and shoulders above everything else, is in the way the House of Commons is made up. We have added another layer to our parliamentary system, in the form of the European Parliament; but we have neither reformed nor even bothered to examine the system itself. I believe our Parliament is too expensive and too numerous; it hogs too much work to itself and is both overcentralized and insufficiently attuned to Brussels and Strasbourg. Bit by bit we should systematically examine our system. We could start by reforming the method of election to the House of Commons, which should reflect the population as a whole. One of the benefits of proportional representation, in my view, would be the strengthening of the centre of politics. The right-wing tail of the Conservative Party has been wagging the dog for some years. It should be sent back to the less than leafy suburb of the Monday Club where it belongs. The extreme left of the Labour Party must be pushed further towards the Socialist Workers' Party, where it belongs. I would like to see two or three parties broadly competing for the centre ground, a pattern seen right across western Europe. That is the essential reform. From that, much else would flow.

We should cut down the number of Members in stages. First we should assess what work they have to do. That is why we have to look at the other elected parts of our system, namely the European Parliament and local government. The goal should be to shed as much work as possible downwards to the directly elected local authorities.

The quangos should be depoliticized, stripped of party appointees. Everyone appointed to the health service should be free from any political taint. They should hold no office nor take any active part, between elections, in any political party. Doctors, nurses and patients should have a say in who is elected to the various boards. In education, likewise, those nominated to posts should be non-party-political standard-bearers. I would go further and work hard to get elected people into local quangos. Only then can there be true public input into the unavoidable debates on expenditure choices.

The House of Lords also needs reform. But I would still keep an element of the hereditary peerage, perhaps as much as one-third of the total membership, for the sake of history and tradition. Hereditary peers could take it in turns to sit in the House, possibly on a three-year cycle, giving way to others at the end of their term. Another third could be nominated life peers, and the remaining third elected on a regional basis. That would allow the House of Lords to reflect the wider European inclination towards strengthening recognition of regional identities. The boundaries of these regions need not conflict with the regions represented in the EU's Committee of the Regions, or with moves towards devolution for Scotland and Wales.

I regard the Government's present tirades against devolution as nothing more than a plea for the continued dominance of a corrupt Parliament at Westminster. John Major is anxious to persuade us all that everything in the British Constitution is fine. Remove the Stone of Scone to Scotland and all is well. These arguments illustrate his distance from the feelings of ordinary people. Westminster urgently needs counterweights. Assemblies in Scotland and Wales could form a valuable part of that process.

If the House of Lords were performing badly at present, I would want more thoroughgoing reform; but it is doing a good job, and there is always room for the kind of wisdom displayed by the specialists and experts in many and varied fields who sit in the present House. The place that's doing badly is the House of Commons. I do, however, object strongly to the present composition of the Lords in one respect, namely that nearly all of the hereditary peerages are reserved for men only. In the modern world I cannot see why this exclusion of women should be tolerated any longer. I would extend that thinking to the Royal Family, so that the Princess Royal could take her rightful place as number two in the family line.

Our present electoral system produces confrontational politics. The arguments sway backwards and forwards from one extreme to another. Today's world is just not like that. There are enough external enemies without having to create internal ones. The world today, especially the better parts of the business world, has found the value of partnership and cooperation. Our system of two lions fighting each other for the spoil is out of time. It is obsolete in other ways, too. The nonsense of ministers coming hot-foot and breathless to declare to the House of Commons some piece of news which has already been declared to the public by the same minister at a press conference or has been on the world news has gone on long enough. Parliament has lost its place as the crucible of the nation. It is the Government's poodle. And as the Government's majority has shrunk, so the methods by which the Executive has retained its grip on backbenchers have sunk closer to the gutter.

The profound sadness which accompanies a process of political disconnection is hard either to imagine or to describe. During the closing stages of my membership of the Conservative Party I found more satisfaction in my voluntary work than in political life. Unfortunately, my political and charitable work constantly crossed paths, and on each occasion the result of this interaction inched me closer to my decision to leave the Party.

John Major's intolerance towards UNESCO stretched my own tolerance for him beyond breaking point in December

1995. UNESCO's Director-General, Dr Federico Mayor, paid a rare visit to London to launch our AMAR/UNESCO Standing Conference, which we entitled 'A Permanent Space for Dialogue'. The objective was to establish and conduct a continuing exploration of the essential hinges which swung the door open or closed between the great European and Islamic civilizations. We planned to concentrate particularly on countries within the European Union (a statistical base) and the Gulf, where the work of the AMAR Appeal had formed the foundation on which we could bring together high-level thinkers on a regular basis to undertake rigorous analysis of the causes of the acute intolerance of Islam I found in so many unexpected places, ranging from the White House to a European Government. Our research was seeking less for commonalities than for differences, its purpose not to create a cosmetic harmony but to recognize dissonance where it exists; only then could enduring and cooperative solutions be developed. We were privileged to have contributions from distinguished academics such as the Khartoum-based Chancellor of the University of Africa, the Head of the Gregorian Institute from Rome, Ayatollah Khamenei's most senior adviser, Ayatollah Taskiri, from Iran, Sheikh Aflah al Rawahy, the Deputy Speaker of the Omani Parliament, and the eminent Saudi businessman Abdullah Alireza. The Archbishop of Canterbury, Dr George Carey, the Director-General of UNESCO, Dr Federico Mayor, and Sheikh Aflah gave the opening speeches. Professor Theodore Zeldin of St Antony's College, Oxford, and other leading academics participated.

The three days were rich with thinking and simple hospitality. The conference coincided with Prince Charles's personal recognition of the plight of Saddam's southern victims. He held a reception at St James's Palace to honour AMAR's work. Among other, wealthier, supporters from the Gulf and Europe were eight hundred schoolchildren, whose commitment was second to none. It was good to see Prince Charles's discussions with his young admirers. The children loved him and they loved the evening; and our intellectuals valued the practical expression of their academic days.

The UN Association, together with Friends of UNESCO, had organized a fiftieth anniversary event on 7 December 1995 to mark the founding of the United Nations itself. (The official celebration of the fiftieth anniversary of UNESCO had been held in Paris two weeks earlier.) Number Ten Downing Street was asked to make a contribution by way of a supportive statement in some way or other. The other notable absentee member from UNESCO was the United States, but President Clinton sent over a magnificent letter which was read out to widespread approbation. He pointed out that the United States endorsed most thoroughly all of the principles of UNESCO and that while he still did not have the budget allocation for rejoining, as Dr Mayor had brought in the proper management disciplines, particularly for financial control, that his predecessor had so badly needed but not imposed, the United States would rejoin as and when the money became available. Contrast that with the stance taken by the Prime Minister of the United Kingdom. A letter was brought to the fiftieth anniversary evening event in the Institute of Engineers just off Parliament Square, the very place where UNESCO had been launched so many years before, by a minister from the House of Lords. It was not an impressive letter. The bearer walked in with it, read it out, and, as hearts dropped like stones, as if to compound the insult to Dr Mayor he declined a seat and departed.

Two hours later, having left our conference, I came to the dinner to be told of this body blow. The room was despondent. The three parliamentary co-chairmen, myself, Mark Fisher (represented by Joan Lestor) and Alex Carlile, were asked to speak. In my few words I told the truth. I was ashamed of the Government's extraordinary discourtesy to someone whose management of UNESCO was widely accepted as one of sparkling creativity. I sat down knowing that I meant every word I had said. Perhaps, without realizing it at the time, I had passed a watershed. Never before had I publicly repudiated the Government in that way.

The previous month I had lunched with Richard Lewartowski, number three in line in ECHO, the European Union humanitarian aid organization. Richard had become a long-standing friend during my four years of struggle to gain help for the Marsh Arabs. His seniors in ECHO were Danato Chiarini, a great Italian, and above him as Director the Spaniard Santiago Gomez-Reino. A British citizen now, Richard came originally from Poland, where his uncle's name was perpetuated in Warsaw on a pavement slab commemorating his young leadership of the bravest of stands against the Nazis' final antisemitic purge. Richard asked me why, in view of the Government's attitude towards overseas aid, and particularly on human rights, asylum legislation and the question of refugees, I still remained Conservative. I answered honestly that in reality it was in unconscious loyalty to my late father. As I went away I wondered whether in fact I was right. I recalled my father's vehement urgings that I should stand up against Mrs Thatcher. I wondered whether or not he would really have wished me to keep in power a Government which was acting against my personal beliefs. Now that he was dead I could never know for sure; but maybe I could release myself from making a judgement on his behalf and using it to block my own perspective.

John Major's penchant for window-dressing found its most dramatic and cynical expression in the Tory leadership election of June 1995. At that time, I still believed in his essential honesty in his dealings with both the parliamentary party and the public and was inclined to support his efforts to keep the party together. After all, he'd been internally elected by a true majority vote. I saw how deviously MPs and party senior volunteers dealt with him on the many occasions when his personal position weakened, as it did in the spring of 1995. They distanced themselves from him in the lobbies, leaving him to walk alone and whispering criticisms behind his back just days after fawning over him publicly. They talked seriously about who was to replace him while offering themselves to him as close friends.

The trouble lay in his own inadequacy as leader. Particularly on Europe, the Prime Minister's preferred tactic for holding the party together seemed to be to give as much ground as possible to both sides of the argument. Whenever he spoke, he was acutely anxious to ensure that he could offer different messages to different audiences and get away with it. He was aided in this by the lack of any first-hand reporting, or any formal record, of the Council of Ministers; this meant that he could, as he was said to have done in Madrid in 1995, say one thing to 'our European partners' (a phrase he used constantly) and another on his return to the House of Commons. Sir Anthony Meyer, who stood against Margaret Thatcher for the party leadership in 1989, recalls that in private conversations he gave 'a very convincing impression of being solidly, though restrainedly, in favour of Europe'; indeed, he notes, 'the phrase "at the heart of Europe" was seldom off his lips'. And yet appeals were constantly made on his behalf, by the Chief Whip and others, to pro-Europeans such as myself, to hold back from making any public statements at all in support of a position that had, after all, been the party's official position since 1971: namely, that Britain's best interests were served by full and active membership of the European Union. Moreover, while we were kept quiet, those who opposed the European concept pushed their argument forward; and the Government consistently gave ground, inch by inch, in the face of this one-sided pressure. Many Conservatives felt betrayed, as I did, by one senior minister after another as we heard them suddenly declare their opposition to policies of great significance that they had supported only weeks earlier. The Chief Whip would not meet the Positive European Group membership.

Meanwhile, the position of the Conservatives in the European Parliament worsened considerably. Some felt that the Conservative Party at home no longer saw them as 'real' Conservatives – a fear validated when those who lost their Strasbourg seats in the 1994 elections attempted to rejoin domestic politics only to find that constituency committees cold-shouldered them. It was indicative of the lack of true seriousness with which the Major Government approached the question of Europe that, as Sir Edward Heath pointed out in the House of Commons during the debate on the intergovernmental confer-ence in March 1996, 'when Parliament debated this country's entry into the Community, it debated for ten full days, and more than 360 of its members took part in those debates,' while in the current debate about 'what may be the most important conference since Messina . . . backbenchers, if lucky, have three hours, at ten minutes each'.

I was as shocked as anyone to hear of John Major's decision to put himself forward for re-election in June 1995. This time I was determined to ensure that some sort of genuine local consultation took place before the vote. John Major had allowed a little more time than Mrs Thatcher did for this to be done; but my new local party chairman begged me to say nothing publicly at all this time round. How, then, could I consult? This cut me off from asking my constituents their views. That sort of consultation, it was made plain, was not desirable; this time, what mattered most was what the local Conservative activists thought. I sent a quick note around while John Redwood and Michael Portillo were squabbling over who should succeed John Major. Redwood got his hat in the ring first, and I knew that a few local activists would have liked me to support him; but his track record was diametrically opposed to my own work for single parents, council house tenants and other poorer members of society. If I were to keep the lowest of profiles requested by my new and hard-working lady chairman, I couldn't criticize John Redwood explicitly, for that would have displayed the split in the Conservative Party which I was being begged not to exacerbate. Instead I wrote a careful letter to the membership suggesting that this time it would be proper to support the Prime Minister, and that party cohesion and unity should take priority over the excitement of change. I could not argue that John Major should be supported because he was the best possible leader, for his record showed this not to be so: he had led Britain nowhere. An appeal to party loyalty, that famous Conservative virtue, was all I could honestly advance. This was mailed out in the normal way to one thousand local party members before the ballot took place.

Had Michael Heseltine or, better still, Kenneth Clarke, come forward, I would unhesitatingly and publicly have supported one of them, but they did not. Heseltine's supporters from last time round had their ears pricked and were waiting for his signal; but it never came, and subsequently the reason for his reticence became apparent. Three weeks before John Major had put himself up for re-election, he had reached an agreement with Michael Heseltine, informally offering him the deputy premiership – the most powerful post of all under a weak Prime Minister – if Heseltine agreed not to contest the election. The appointment was confirmed on the day of the contest.

Seeing John Major's misery as he decided to put his name forward, and the way in which, over the previous months, previous boot-lickers had been turning their kicks on him, I told him that I would continue to give him my support. After all, I had accepted the post of Parliamentary Private Secretary; if I wasn't prepared to support him I should drop that small task. A campaigning office was set up in Cowley Street, just opposite the Liberal Democrat offices. I went round to offer assistance, but it wasn't wanted. The eight or so ministers and activists in the room looked almost upset at having an offer of help. It was clear that they were marking their cards for future promotion. For most of them, this strategy worked; and, after all, for advancement they were wholly dependent upon the system of favours. Around the corner there was another campaign office, unknown to the official one. This was in Alastair Goodlad's house, where perhaps the real shots were being called. He subsequently became Chief Whip.

My brief local note did the trick: the party membership knew precisely what I was doing but without the publicity that my party chairman would have found so unwelcome. I resolved to maintain this low profile right up to the ballot box and make my vote a secret one. I arrived in Committee Room corridor around midday, a couple of hours after the ballot had opened, intending to get voting out of the way early. I found a shambles. A seething mass of journalists blocked both doorways, in and out of the Committee Room, and the passage as well. It was chaos. I learned that the chairman of the 1922 Committee, Sir Marcus Fox, had been criticized earlier for running an open ballot instead of a secret one and had let the press in suddenly to show them that the vote was indeed secret. I entered the room and found the most open quasi-secret ballot I had ever seen. Sir Marcus had a couple of people with him to monitor the voting; the table for marking the ballot papers was right in front of them and the ballot box was very close. The minister in front of me knew precisely what he was expected to do, and did it. He sat down in the marking place – the only one available – and marked his paper clearly in front of Sir Marcus and his colleagues, declaring, rather unnecessarily, that he was supporting John Major, of course, and wasn't this a waste of time. He folded his paper, strolled back to the box and pushed it in. To show my disapproval of this charade, I inched behind the ballot box and marked my paper there. The anger of the organizers at my semi-secrecy was plain: three furious pop-eyed faces swivelled and stared at me as I left.

Chapter 12

Crossing the Floor

Alan Howarth's resignation of the Conservative Party whip in October 1995 seemed to me to stem from several speeches he made in the spring and summer that year, against the Government's position on both the unemployed and the disabled. The strength and passion of his pleading struck me as marking fundamental change within him. It was really no surprise to me when, as Parliament started to reassemble after the conference season, it was declared that he was joining the Labour Party. I was very sorry that we were no longer to be in the same party, but I fully appreciated his reasons and sympathized with them. I had apologized to him for not supporting him in the Division Lobby earlier in the summer, but both he and I knew the constraints on me while I remained a PPS. Perhaps I was surprised that he had chosen to go to the Labour Party, since I had felt that his views fitted him more properly for the Liberal Democrat benches; but that was his choice and I respected it.

His move left me with an embarrassment. In May I had accepted, on his repeated personal urging, an invitation from his constituency association to speak at their annual lunch, clearly an important occasion, in late October. The date was now rapidly approaching, and I knew what would be demanded under the circumstances: no less than a demolition of his position, not just recently but throughout his whole career. Public execution was what the Conservative Party demanded in such circumstances, and I would not be willing to carry out that task. It would perhaps be better if I withdrew.

I asked a local party official in Devon what would be the neatest way of extricating myself from the engagement. I also sent a note to Alan saying that I was sure he would not wish me to appear in the circumstances. Responses to both were rapid. Conservative Central Office, immediately alerted by Devon, sent a message to say that it was imperative I went, else they would doubt me too. More importantly to me, Alan himself telephoned and pleaded with me to keep the engagement. Even now, he did not want to let his constituency down.

I gave in. On Friday 20 October I travelled to Warwick, where I was picked up by a couple proudly displaying a badge bearing the message 'Hang Howarth' beside a picture of a noose. This, I heard, had been handed out at the party conference – the first since the late 1970s that I had not attended. At the lunch itself the agent, with an air of great triumph, raffled a bottle of gin called 'Traitor's Gate', and people begged me to wear the 'Hang Howarth' badge. In my speech I asked those present to understand why Alan had moved. I suggested that maybe they had not lost him altogether and that he would continue to serve the constituency; I even tried to cheer them up by suggesting he might return to them, though I thought it unlikely. Some agreed with me, but others were very angry; my plea for understanding fell on stony ground. Altogether it was a dismal occasion.

After the lunch John Pienaar, the knowledgeable BBC lobby correspondent, caught me for a brief interview. He and his camera crew were there to see if they could get a sense of who might replace Alan as Conservative candidate. He challenged me on my unhappiness at the occasion, and I told him why I was so ill at ease with it. He asked if I would move too, and pursued me on the point in the next couple of months. I begged him to leave me alone; I said that if I were to have to make such a difficult decision, I would make it alone. In return for privacy, I said, I would promise to come to him exclusively if I were to take such a step.

In the meantime the Nolan vote came and went, leaving a lingering unpleasantness in the air. On 8 December, the last day of our AMAR/UNESCO European Union Islamic conference, I received a message from one of Michael's closest colleagues in the Booker world just as we were about to begin work. He had just lunched with the Liberal Democrat peer Richard Holme and wanted to pass on the message that Richard, who had never met me, would enjoy a political discussion some time. The messenger added that this was not his business, but that, if requested, he could pass a message back. I thought about it. Richard has a serious political mind. I had half regretted not knowing him, but our political paths just had not crossed. I checked with Michael; he too had read Richard's work and warmed to his academically thoughtful approach to politics.

The conference wound up and the weekend came, packed with a variety of work and a little political campaigning. I was gearing myself up for the Christmas constituency round of visits to hospitals, police and fire stations, old people's homes and those over-stressed bearers of Christmas, the postmen and women. I also had it in mind to write a letter to Matthew Owen, briefly my Liberal Democrat opponent in Devon West and Torridge. He was a young man and his family needs – the birth of their first child – had made him regretfully withdraw from the seat. But I didn't want a letter of support for his decision to be misinterpreted as a political rebuke, and I thought that if I sent it to Liberal Democrat head office, it might perhaps be opened in error. Even in my own office, envelopes marked 'private and confidential' are sometimes ripped open in haste. I needed his home address, but since the death of his father, the former Chief Education Officer at County Hall and a friend, I had no easy method of tracking him down. Perhaps a Liberal Democrat Member of Parliament could help. I also recognized within myself a deeper feeling that a discussion with a senior Liberal Democrat would be a welcome chance to share political thoughts. Colleagues on the

Conservative side who thought as I did were utterly dismayed by Government actions. They readily agreed with the views I had held for months, even years. But we were powerless; or, worse, our shared and individual efforts to influence our Government, our Whips, our 1922 Committee fell on such stony ground that they produced negative results.

I went to a meeting with the Local Government Commissioners as a last-ditch attempt to gain independent local government status for Exeter, something the city had lost in 1974. Throughout the summer I had strenuously fought against other Devon County colleagues who were opposing Rupert Allason's campaign for a unitary authority for Torbay. A triumvirate of unitary authorities for Devon would release the rural areas to be taken seriously once more. For me a resumption of the rural district council structure was the best solution; city unitary authorities would achieve the same result under a different name. Only John Hannam, the Exeter Member, Nick Harvey, the Liberal Democrat for Devon North, and I were there. Nick Harvey's argument and my own had a commonality that was immediately recognizable.

I thought about it afterwards. This was not just a shared purpose born from the close similarity of our two constituencies. I sensed a deeper common approach, something I had also noted working with Alex Carlile on the difficult UN Committee for Tolerance, and so often in speeches given by Paul Tyler, next door to me now in Cornwall North, and in Matthew Taylor's work further down the peninsula in Truro. I had never found myself differing from either David Steel or Alan Beith, and I had been ashamed of the shabby behaviour of the Conservatives who jeered at Paddy Ashdown when he talked such consistent sense on Bosnia. Robert Maclennan was wise and sensible, and I had always counted Menzies Campbell of Fife North East a political heavyweight, with views similar to my own. Charles Kennedy was very bright, and when campaigning in the West of Scotland I had warmed towards

Ray Michie for her dedicated constituency work. I had spent almost the whole of one night on that Scottish campaign tour trying to straighten out the rabid right-wing thinking of the Scottish Young Conservatives. I left them at three in the morning and returned to the charge at seven. We parted friends, and I had made some converts to the cause of generous thinking towards one's fellow men when they disarmingly told me that never before had any senior Conservative discussed any matters of political principle with them. I was not surprised; it had been a very wearing night. However, the fact remained that these were the young members of the Conservative Party entitled to carry that banner. Their views, as I saw subsequently from the flavour of Michael Portillo's anti-Brussels conference speech and the smell of prejudice and racism arising from Conservative pressure groups, were becoming mainstream.

I could not stay as a Conservative. I had known this, and told Michael, since the Nolan vote in November. Should I walk out quietly, as many people had already done in 1992, and many more since? Or should I take the Chiltern Hundreds and cause a by-election? At least this latter course would give me a more constructive future earlier, helping my fellow men and women instead of hindering them. Christmas was approaching. Why not just leave, I asked myself? The answer became apparent: because I wanted the Government to fall. I believed their actions had become pernicious. Far from desiring the greatest good for the greatest number of people and acting in accordance with that common aim, they wanted to hurt, not to heal; to crush, not to be compassionate with the weakest. Poison had entered the heart of the Government. Their huge confidence lay only in a self-perceived right to govern, a cardinal falsehood in a democratic system. Opposing the Government as an independent Conservative would be ineffectual. All I could deliver from that position was an occasional glancing blow that the Government would never heed. If I wanted the Government to fall there was a proper place in Parliament from which to work on a consistent basis, with others who agreed with that goal. That place was the Opposition benches.

This could not mean the Labour benches, despite cajoling messages from Labour friends and despite my recognition of their worth. Later, after I had joined the Liberal Democrats, the Labour Women's Group upbraided me gently: why hadn't I come on further, to them? Everyone in the Commons knew how much I disagreed with most of the Government's actions and they would have welcomed me into their group; I could have become a Labour Member. But for me, as for Mrs Thatcher, socialism had always been the enemy. Even she could not be persuaded really to fight against the Liberals. Actually that suited me, because in those days my political ferocity was reserved for socialism as practised by the British Labour Party. I had always found it very difficult indeed to sustain an intellectual argument against the Liberals or the SDP. Since then, the New Model Labour Party had made strides in seven-league boots; but it still carried with it the baggage of a century of socialist thinking. That was not for me. The only possibility lay with the Liberal Democrats. I had to talk to them. Maybe I wouldn't fit them and maybe they wouldn't fit me, but one thing was clear: I had to find out.

But how? That was the difficulty: there were so few Liberal Democrat Members, and they were so busy. In mid-December I went up to one or two in the Members' Lobby with suitable questions to ask on impartial matters, but they had vanished before I could establish a conversation. In any case, to start a substantive discussion in the Members' Lobby would be lunacy. Since Alan Howarth's departure the Whips had been cosseting me in a ludicrous way quite unlike any treatment I had had from them before. One had even put his arm around my waist and wished me happy birthday. He'd also urged me to turn to the right. Beneath the forced bonhomie, they seemed to be monitoring every breath I took. An instance of this in December bewildered me. I was invited to lunch with the wife of a Whip who, quite transparently, was acting as an agent of the Office. The clumsiness and feebleness of this approach distressed me, and only reinforced my feeling of being quite out of place in the Conservative Party.

I could, however, quite properly approach Nick Harvey, since he was my constituency next-door neighbour and we could easily have local matters to discuss. I chose my moment carefully and, catching him alone in a corridor, asked about Matthew Owen. He said of course he would give me his address, he was sure Matthew would be delighted to get a letter, and yes, indeed, Matthew's action was right, it was almost impossible to combine the time and travel demands of being a parliamentary candidate with having a very young family. I paused. He asked how I was. I dropped my guard totally, replying honestly and with complete frankness that I was politically immensely unhappy. The Conservative Government was wrong in its policies and its actions, both for myself and for my constituents. Teasingly, he said: 'Why not join us?' I threw down my gauntlet, replying, 'Because you haven't asked me. Maybe I would if you did.' Startled, he disappeared.

I tried to contact him again, but it was not possible. Christmas was just too close and the House was about to rise. I chose the other route, sending a message back through Michael's colleage to Richard Holme, accepting a meeting and seeking an appointment. On 19 December, I had an early breakfast with him in his office off St James's Square. Despite sneezing heavily with a bad cold, he was courteous, diplomatic, unpressing; we talked sociably for twenty minutes about shared friends. My time was nearly up, and we both had work to do. I raised the question of the Liberal Democrat approach to the European Union. Immediately he came to life. Our meeting concluded after a further ten minutes, but our discussions had only just begun. On the twenty-first he gave me tea in the Meridien Hotel, Piccadilly, against the background of a professional harpist keeping the Japanese tourists happy. It was apparent from our conversation that my views on the European Union were the same as those carried forward by the Liberal Democrats. On other issues that we touched on, too, it was as hard to see the difference between myself and them as it had been easy for colleagues on all sides of the House of Commons to see the gulf between myself and the Government. I suggested a third talk. Richard said that really if I wanted to talk further it should be with Paddy Ashdown, and he gave me the party leader's number. I called him and we had tea on 23 December somewhere in North Devon. Again, the shared political perspective became clear immediately. What was also apparent was his grasp of political realities, which the Conservative Party had lost; and, again in contrast, his leadership qualities.

Christmas intervened and with it all the familiar activity: stockings, plum pudding, Christmas crackers and paper hats with Amar, my nieces, nephews, sisters, brothers-in-law and other family connections. There was no time for political discussion, nor did I want there to be; this was a personal dark night. Then I returned to London, telling Michael that I had to make up my political mind, I could wait no longer.

The following morning I telephoned Paddy and in the evening asked him if I might join the Liberal Democrats. The next day I met him again, this time with a very different sort of Chief Whip, Archie Kirkwood, and Alan Leaman, director of strategy and planning. After two days of intense activity I announced my decision publicly in an interview for the BBC *Nine o'Clock News*. John Pienaar, to whom I paid this debt, turned out to be watching cricket in South Africa, so I spoke to Robin Oakley, the BBC's political editor. To him I said:

> I have moved because I have reached the end of the road
> with the Conservatives. The Liberal Democrats concep-
> tualize my own personal philosophy and feelings in a way
> the Conservative Party no longer does: concern for the

poor, for people in trouble, both those at home and those seeking asylum; and, over and above all, a straightforward goal on Europe – namely, involvement as hard and as fast as we possibly can, for the sake of Britain and everybody else – and equally a vision of Britain's future. All this is sorely missing from the Conservative Government.

The Conservative Party has changed so much, while my principles have not changed at all. I would argue that it is not so much a case of my leaving the party, but the party leaving me. The Conservative Party has shifted and I think there are thousands if not millions of people who are or have been Conservative voters who sadly agree with me. As a Member of Parliament I have to use my vote, and I have become very miserable using it in favour of statements and measures with which I profoundly disagreed. The Conservative Party is no longer the One Nation party I joined. It's become sectional, fragmented, angry – angry with specific parts of the nation, single mothers, asylum-seekers, people from ethnic minorities, people of different religions.

The time has come to be honest with myself and honest with the electorate and to change sides. I have chosen to change to the Liberal Democrats because their philosophy is so akin to mine, and they have been kind enough to welcome me. In fact, I wonder why I haven't been with them all along.

I was reminded of Nelson Mandela's description of freedom: 'To be free is not merely to cast off one's chains, but to live in a way that respects and enhances the freedom of others.'

Entering the House of Commons as a Liberal Democrat for the first time was a surprisingly comfortable experience. I walked with my new colleagues into St Stephen's entrance, past a vast bank of photographers and up into Central Lobby. We passed through the Members' Lobby and went into the Liberal

Democrat Whips' Office. Robert Maclennan and Archie Kirkwood led me in and I found a batch of welcoming faces waiting to greet me. It should have felt odd to be one of them, to be mixing with those opposite whom I had sat for so long. But it simply didn't. I felt the slight awkwardness that goes with being a new entrant into a well-oiled team; but in political terms, I felt at ease. I felt as if the metal box of Conservative constraint had fallen away and I was free politically to explore fresh ideas.

At 2.28 p.m., a minute before Madam Speaker led her retinue into the Members' Lobby between black-clad Palace servants, we walked into the Chamber. I turned to the right instead of to the left, slipped into my new benches and sat down. Madam Speaker was announced and we all stood and went through the familiar parliamentary prayers. I felt a particular identity with the Prayer for Parliamentarians, that three- to four-hundred-year-old call to Members to set aside their personal ambitions and work for the good of the people.

On that first afternoon in the Chamber as a Liberal Democrat, I felt the wrath of the Government side in the hostile glares directed at me across the floor. Their anger was intensified by the welcome I received from the Opposition Members. I was already among the Liberal Democrats when the first Labour Member to congratulate me offered his hand: it was the Chief Whip, Donald Dewar, one of the nicest and most honourable of men. And so it went on.

For the remainder of January the Conservative Party shifted and twisted in its attempts to curb my speeches. I spoke on asylum legislation. They got hold of a copy of my draft thoughts and circulated it within the Chamber on the Conservative side. When I stood up they screamed that I was reading and should be stopped. Madam Deputy Speaker, the calm and elegant Janet Fookes of Plymouth, rebuked the critics, saying that if their objection held good then most Members would have most of their speeches scrapped. Nearly everybody uses some form of note from which to talk. They bellowed throughout my speech, and in his reply the minister, Jeremy Hanley, picked a comment from my draft that I had not put on the record, and lambasted it.

Led by David Nicholson, trying to stave off his own looming electoral defeat, Conservative Members got to work on the note I had sent round to party activists within my constituency the previous June, at the time of the leadership election. This short note achieved a wide but partial publication when sentences were stripped from context and used by John Major and Michael Heseltine, in the Chamber, and by David Nicholson and other former colleagues in an early day motion. Even the new (and unsuccessful) Conservative newspaper picked it up. First the sentences were used to claim that I was a Conservative Party worshipper; then, as the months went by, my attackers' imaginative reporting efforts grew and my few words of June 1995 were trumpeted as 'my own election message'. They must have thought I'd issued it in 1992, at the last general election.

From the Despatch Box, surely wasting parliamentary time, John Major and his ministers launched a stream of attacks at me. The House of Commons police somehow know everything. Minutes after one particularly vicious barracking from my former colleagues I emerged from the Chamber and, as I walked past three of them, one said cheerfully: 'You stand up to them, don't be put down, you're not going back, you got it right. They'll soon give up.' Sure enough, the Prime Minister's own side told him and other ministers to tone down their attacks since they were proving so counter-productive. Public sympathy was with me, borne out by the Liberal Democrats' standing in the polls. As a taxi driver remarked to me later, only the Conservative Party could use 'integrity' as a dirty word. So the Prime Minister changed tack and said how bitterly I would regret my decision. His second-guessing of my future feelings proved as erroneous as many of his other judgements on larger matters. It was the best decision of my political life.

The Conservative Party were instructed not to speak to me, to send me to Coventry in best boys' prep school style. This had some bizarre effects. I met at dinner a minister for whom I had worked. We were on public duty, assisting in giving hospitality for the Secretary-General of the United Nations, Dr Boutros Boutros Ghali. It was odd to find him staring through me when only a few weeks earlier I had helped him on some work. The minister for whom I had served as PPS, Michael Jack, did just the same. They all did. Sir John Spicer, another former Party Vice-Chairman (under John Gummer) had a long discussion with me at a formal lunch after I had left the party; he was cheerful and friendly. He then spoke on the BBC's *Sunday* programme, declaring that I was 'a non-person' and he was never going to speak to me again. He must have thought he was lunching with a ghost. In private letters, of course, they still sought my help on unfinished matters of particular business, and added nice comments; but whether within the Chamber or outside at embassy lunches, they behaved as if those letters had never been written, and indeed as if I did not exist. I assumed that this was how they treated the office cleaners, as they certainly appeared to have had plenty of practice at it. In fact, I found it a rather comfortable position.

A northern Member sent a press release to his local newspaper saying that he had written to me, that I had replied, and that he would be releasing the text of my letter to the newspaper and challenging me on its content the next time he saw me in the Commons. Neither his letter nor mine existed; nor has he spoken to me since.

The ultimate in fanciful thinking came from Michael Heseltine, who claimed that I had been to see him twice recently in the House of Commons to talk about a job in Government. This was not true. Late one night in November 1995 I had stopped him in a passage at the House to talk about his not standing for the leadership this time around, having had a note from him not long previously telling me once more that I had voted the right way, that is to say against John Major in the second ballot, in 1990. At the end of our few seconds of conversation, I reminded him that eighteen months earlier he had said that he would let me know what lay behind the curious hot/cold treatment I was getting from the party hierarchy, the repeated suggestions that I was about to be offered a Government post, which were never followed up. This was not mere curiosity. I was beginning to plan for a possible career outside Parliament if – as many honorary officials in my constituency were telling me – we were to lose the seat in the next election, and with this possibility in mind I had already been to see a senior head-hunter in London, a friend of Michael's, for an informal talk. He had told me that in seeking future employment I must focus my thinking specifically on what I was good at and identify where my weaknesses lay. With the thoroughness I had learned in business, I had set about gathering this information, and knowing what my perceived weaknesses were in the minds of my colleagues was clearly a vital part of the picture. My discussion with Michael Heseltine on this occasion did not last, end to end, more than a few minutes; and most of it was spent talking about his future, not mine. Later that same month, on 24 November, Mr Heseltine came to my constituency. Conservative Central Office were so anxious about the weakness of the party's hold on the seat that they sent down four ministers in quick succession that autumn; Michael Heseltine was the third to appear. We spoke again briefly.

Following these two meetings he built a wall of assaults on me in the New Year, claiming that I had had meetings with him in the Commons and had asked him for a Government job. It seemed he had confused his time-scales. I had asked him for no job at all since 1990, when I had indeed asked if I could be his PPS. The manner of his refusal on that occasion was so discourteous that I resolved at the time never to ask him for a job again. Nor did I.

None of the ministers who visited my constituency that autumn greatly helped the local supporters of the Conservative cause. All of them, including Nicholas Lyell, delivered great perorations, building up attack after attack upon New Labour, claiming that it was no different from Old Labour, that its policies were identical and that it was a frightening spectre. This took up nine-tenths of their speaking time – except for William Waldegrave, who gave some erudite analysis of the immediate past budget as well. When it came to the crunch, instead of setting out the reasons for voting for the party, they merely appealed for the audience's support on the basis that the Conservatives had the right to rule. There was no explanation of why the country should support the ruling party, merely the statement that they held the reins of power and should continue to do so.

Despite ministerial reluctance to engage in proper political discourse, I still retained a shred of hope that, although all the evidence suggested otherwise, the Government would have its reasons for pursuing overtly antipathetic policies; and, having made my decision and left the party, I anticipated that the Government would demolish my reasons for resigning the whip within hours, if not minutes. They had the data: stacks of it, filing cabinets and computer memories full of it, and I was a mere backbencher, outside the circle of real knowledge. I thought that, once they had grasped the points I was making – and I made them very clearly indeed, first on the *Nine o'Clock News*, then on ITN's *The World Tonight* and the following morning in the *Western Morning News* – they would pounce on and demolish my political arguments in the twinkling of an eye.

That they did not do this, but chose instead to attack me as a person, represented to me their ultimate acknowledgement of failure to govern to proper standards. I should have known that the Government would prefer to blame me personally rather than address its political failures: after all, this was what they had been doing with increasing frequency in the previous months and years, shifting blame sideways, very deliberately and with a good helping of inaccuracies, on to those nearest at hand. BSE? Blame the famers for feeding the wrong food to the animals. Forget the fact that farmers had persisently called for mandatory labelling of feedstuffs. Arms to Iraq? Quickly blame the Opposition leaders for criticizing the Government; never mind the fact that Government ministers had misled Parliament. Women in labour chained up in prison hospitals? Blame the newspapers for raising a scare, and say it isn't true; when another medium, Channel Four Television, shows smuggled film demonstrating the validity of the allegation, blame the prison governor or the civil servants for not showing the minister the relevant letters. Blame the system for a failure of information. Never take the trouble to acquire the information by actually going to the hospital or prison, talking to the prisoners or the governor.

And so it was with me. The Government failures I listed in my statements after leaving the party – on education, on the National Health Service, on the treatment of vulnerable members of society, on asylum-seekers, on the complete failure of leadership on European issues: all were ignored, and I was targeted severally and together as a menopausal political prostitute, a bitch with a boring voice and boundless, if thwarted, ambition.

I had vowed that I would not respond by repeating private conversations, although I had plenty of material to hand which would have tarnished my accusers, sometimes with politically fatal results. Instead, I tried hard to stick to the political ground, since that was what the argument should have been all about. The personal insults bounced off me, partly because they seemed so inappropriate. One later apologized for his unpleasant personal comments and said that he knew I would take them as a joke. It hadn't been a joke at the time, but I forbore to say so; what was the point? These men were trivial even in their approach to matters of real substance. Their technique didn't work. It broke down largely because it was ineffectual. I made no secret of my personal weaknesses, inconsistencies and less than perfect thinking. It was because what I had said about the Government's performance was true that the public agreed with me.

In the Commons I stayed away from those Conservative Members whom I had long admired and whose worth had largely been ignored by successive party leaders. Peter Temple-Morris, Patrick Cormack, Anthony Steen, Peter Bottomley, Tim Rathbone, George Walden, Robert Hicks, David Harris, Roger Sims, Patrick Thompson – there were many of them, eminent men who should surely have made a lasting contribution to the government of the country. Perhaps they had been left out because their tolerance and understanding of society's complex needs had precluded adherence to the ideological tenets of the rightward-moving party; they were deemed 'too soft'. I retained my respect for their work, wherever I sat in the House of Commons. Underneath our exterior divisions, we shared a common goal, the good of the people. Perhaps, like me, they were privately dubbed 'welfare MPs', a label that only political extremists such as those on the Conservative right wing could use as a term of political abuse.

I still have many friends in the Conservative Party whose work I respect and, in some cases, even admire. Some of them are silent about the Conservative excesses of the sort that I have accurately described. Some are leaving because of their own unease at what is taking place. Fifty-six Tory MPs stood down at the 1992 election, against forty-three in 1987 and thirty-three in 1983; at July 1996, possibly ten months before the next election, fifty-four had already announced their intention to stand down, a figure that would surely rise. A few, most notably Peter Thurnham, have taken sterner action, although none save Alan Howarth, whose move preceded my own, have taken the final step. Their circumstances are not mine. I owed no debt to anyone and was therefore free to make my choice. My good fortune lay in the existence of the Liberal Democrats. Although I respect New Labour, had the Liberal Democrat Party not existed I would have sought no other political colour. Their cause became mine; because, unnoticed by me, it had in reality been my own cause all along.

It is salutary in terms of human behaviour to see how the growth of the Conservative parliamentary party's present culture of supporting many members' personal and financial gains at the expense of their constituents and the public has drawn so many honourable people through the wrong lobbies. I must have been guilty of that myself on many occasions. As I wrote to John Major on my departure, I had 'supported the Government in every whipped vote, under both Margaret Thatcher and yourself, and every unwhipped vote when requested to do so during my years as a Parliamentary Private Secretary. However, my conviction is now that I would be wrong in terms of my principles, the interests of my constituents and the future of the country to continue that pattern of voting.' I felt it important to identify the system which, unless a Member fully breaks away, imperceptibly corrupts their judgement through the insistent pressures of the whipping system. But I received no reply.

In the final weeks before I left the Conservative Party I had made a huge effort to get through to Kenneth Clarke, who, with his vision of a future, more tolerant Conservative Government, was probably the only minister who could, at that late stage, have kept me within the party. I had left a number of messages for him, without result. It was impossible to catch a busy Chancellor's elbow, eye or ear by any of the normal means. Eventually, in desperation, I had sent a clear shout for help through one of his closer colleagues, asking if I could meet with him to discuss my future in the Conservative Party. It was the only acceptable coded message that I could use. This final effort failed; I doubt whether it even reached him.

My views of Kenneth Clarke, and of other ministers, remained unaltered after I had left the party. I continued to admire the Chancellor's work and to be dismayed by the negative attitudes of Peter Lilley, Michael Howard and other members of the Government towards our society. What was new to me from my position on the Liberal Democrat benches was the sight of their faces in Question Time and during debates. Sitting for so long behind them, I had never seen them face to face as they spoke; watching their expressions now gave me the uncanny feeling that these were not people I should ever have followed. In the asylum debate in June 1996, a Scottish Nationalist woman Member mentioned rape, asking how a woman having suffered this offence would rank in an entry clearance officer's assessment of her as an asylum-seeker. First Timothy Kirkwood, the minister in charge of asylum matters, then Peter Lilley, the Whip Roger Knapman, and others along the Government bench started to laugh. I had noticed Home Office ministers behaving similarly when the matter of women prisoners giving birth in hospital had been raised. These people were unsuitable to govern in a civilized society.

At the end of January 1996, when the *Daily Telegraph* was still searching around for words to twist against me, I learned the hard way that newspaper ownership now dominates the journalists' output. Their reporters told me that even they were astonished at the intensity, duration and ferocity of the personal campaign being waged against me. They were receiving calls from Conservative Central Office every day, often many times a day, urging them on to do everything possible to destroy me. My saddest encounter with the *Telegraph* came early in January. In response to the frantic urging of the features editor, I agreed to a profile interview by one of their major writers. I was then told it was urgent and had to be done within a few days, and that I should know that the journalist in question had had heavy chemotherapy treatment for cancer and was in appalling health. Could I be really kind to him? I was; both Michael and I took enormous care to settle him comfortably, look after him and answer his questions (we'd been asked to do it as fully and carefully as possible). He even had difficulty with his microphone and asked me to speak particularly loudly to help him, which, of course, I did.

The article that eventually emerged bore scant relation to the interview. It was a calculated smear, including five major factual errors that could readily have been checked, even in *Who's Who*. Laughably, it criticized my 'power' dressing, my large brooch and huge earrings, my padded shoulders, while the very photograph they used would have shown him that I wore no brooch, simple stud earrings and an old tweed jacket. More hurtful was the writer's unpleasant comment on the loudness of my voice and how unattractive he had found it (voice production is difficult for everyone with hearing difficulties). So much for the problems with his tape recorder.

The *Daily Mail*, after an early and accurate report about why I had left the Conservative Party, turned their fire upon Michael's first wife. She, an elderly lady now living in isolation in rural France, rang up in a most miserable state to report that four *Daily Mail* journalists were camping around her house and men from the *Daily Express* and the *Sun* were in the vicinity. She could not get them to go. They stayed for four days, badgering her. Despite their harassment she gave little ground and was constantly on the telephone to us. The article the *Mail* journalists subsequently produced could have been created from their press cuttings from the time when Michael parted from his wife, thirteen years earlier. She had made an unguarded remark then, which she subsequently regretted, that the *Mail* chose to enlarge upon. Michael had not responded. It would have been discourteous to her to do so.

The *Sun*, for its part, dug out a letter that I had written, modifying a draft from Central Office, significantly nearly a year before. Conservative Central Office had decided that seats that might be difficult to keep at the next election should send out survey letters. This was an expensive game and I wasn't sure that it would be much help. It cost my agent bitter hours of work in entering names and addresses and other data into his word processor as the forms were returned. It was a standard letter and a pretty dull one; written in the autumn of 1994, it was mailed out, over a printed signature once I had agreed it, from February 1995 onwards. The *Sun* brandished a copy that had been sent to someone by my agent in about November, claiming this showed I was two-faced. This seemed a very shaky claim to me. After all, I didn't make my mind up to leave the Conservative Party until late December, and I was still trying to promote the best of the old style of Conservative message right up until Christmas.

In the constituency, the *Western Morning News* ran my article the day after my television interview, and followed it up with some straightforward pieces. The following weekend the tone changed and I was attacked. Television stations reacted locally in slightly different ways. An unprofessional note was struck by Television Southwest when they invited me for a one-to-one discussion in Plymouth and, once I was in the studio, faced me with a local activist. Curiously, this was someone who had written to me just before Christmas in despair about the centralizing record of the Conservative Government; yet here he was attacking me in public just ten days later as if he had been a hard-line supporter of the Government all along. It put me off balance as, while he was clearly quite prepared to launch unpleasant personal criticism at me, I just didn't feel that I could respond in the same way, though I had much the more powerful ammunition. His performance made me rather sad.

Few of the local Conservatives replied to my letters to them. I had hoped that some would be willing to discuss their attitudes. I knew that a lot of them agreed with my views and had been telling me of their deep dissatisfaction with the Conservative Party for many, many months. Even if they disagreed with the line I had taken, at least we would understand each other and could part friends. But some turned out to be worse than bad losers. In June 1996 I was asked to speak in Tiverton parish church on the occasion of the three hundredth anniversary of their famous organ, housed in a casing made by Grinling Gibbons. A local Conservative councillor wrote to the Tiverton newspaper, bitterly complaining that I was coming to speak in his church. Venomous, anonymous – but clearly Conservative – callers made such vicious threats down the telephone that the vicar had to call Special Branch.

One member of the congregation was Mary, Lady O'Hagan, former wife of the Conservative MEP for Devon, Charles O'Hagan. She wrote afterwards, repelled by this behaviour:

'Many people like me, growing up during the Cold War and holding distinctly centrist views on domestic policy, backed the Conservatives out of a desire to oppose appeasement of Russia and to support European integration. That was then. Pouring self-serving vitriol on our closest neighbours and threatening the freedom of speech and even the physical safety of a former Conservative MP appears to be the Conservative Party now. I want none of it. To think that two centuries of spectacular political success have resulted in this. It is sad beyond words.'

Some of those who had taken particular pleasure in claiming my friendship and to whom I had offered genuine personal support and hospitality, severed the connection once I was of no use to them and their political careers. On the other hand, the enormous gratitude that thousands of people expressed to me by letter, on the telephone and in person, in villages and towns, on trains, aeroplanes, buses and the London Tube, in shops and in the House of Commons, was overwhelming. It went on and on: no day passed in my first six months as a Liberal Democrat without somebody stopping me somewhere and thanking me for having stood up to the Government. It seemed that people felt the Government was all-powerful and far from benign towards them. There was a deep unease at the way in which Government was taking away freedom of action from individuals and communities; and people felt that there was nothing they could do to stop this, since so many channels of communication had been blocked off, so many methods of influencing decisions removed. The Government had sucked them in, and absorbed them. The checks and balances had progressively disappeared.

As I settled down to answer my many letters, I did some research on movements across the House of Commons in earlier times. About 230 Members had crossed the floor in living memory. Very few had resigned their seats, causing by-elections. One who had was Tony Benn's father: hence his fiercely rigid view that those who resigned the Whip should always stand down. I tried to argue with him on this but he wouldn't listen. My point was simple: that the independence of Members of Parliament was something to be prized. In the modern democratic political system in the United Kingdom, the role of individual judgement has almost been squeezed out. The party system has become so strong and the Government's enlargement of the Executive so relentless that on the Conservative side nearly one Member of Parliament in two is in Government employment. On top of that, the MP's salary is for many their family's main or only source of income. Some MPs appear to manage take-home pay of over £100,000 a year by dint of passing the secretarial allowance straight on to their wives and working the system in other ways. But even for those honourable enough to submit more modest claims, the £43,000 salary is crucial. Members of Parliament are self-employed. If they resign their seats, they can make few financial claims on the state. The result is that if MPs are forced to stand down when they change parties, no one will ever do so again. That final assurance that the public has of a Member of Parliament's individual judgement will be taken away.

Devon and Cornwall had already seen a substantial number of their Members cross the floor of the House of Commons.

Indeed, in my own constituency of Devon West and Torridge and the two neighbouring ones of Plymouth and Devon North, seven Members of Parliament had done so this century. Perhaps they, like me, had realized that the Government and Whitehall no longer cared for their constituents' future and so sought another way of influencing the political debate.

After my move to the Liberal Democrats I had cause to meet the recently appointed education minister, Cheryl Gillan, on constituency business. I introduced her to Peter Upton, head teacher of Tavistock Community College, and she claimed that the school's buildings problem, stretching back over years, was the fault of the Liberal Democrats in the County Council. I had to remind her that, until eight months previously, the Conservative Party had been in charge ever since the local government reorganization of 1974.

Underlying the practice of democracy in Britain is the unwritten belief, reflected in parliamentary practices, that the opposing viewpoint to that of the Government is worthy of respect. As the duty of a Government is to govern, so the duty of the Opposition, official and otherwise, must be to oppose. A succession of parliamentary rights have accrued to those who disagree with the Government's view. At the time of the Civil Wars in the seventeenth century, Speaker Lethbridge opposed King Charles in refusing to allow him to chase 'the birds [which had] flown', namely those MPs who were opposed to the King's views and had left the House of Commons before Charles and his armed men forced entry. Today the Executive is in the House of Commons, and so is the Opposition. Unfortunately, the right to oppose is not encapsulated in a formal document in Britain. There is no written constitution, and since Parliament is above the law and the House of Commons an omnipotent body, Parliament's own unwritten *modus operandi* does not provide any legal protection. Take the Government's treatment of the Opposition in the case of the Scott Report. Lord Justice Scott concluded that William Waldegrave had misled

Parliament, and the Government perceived this to be an attack on its position. It therefore used every possible device to hamper the Opposition's ability to deal constructively with Sir Richard's findings on the day of their official publication. First, the Government delayed full publication of the report by two full weeks, during which time a private publication for Government alone took place. It spent those two weeks sifting the report and working out ways of massaging the most damaging aspects. Second, it allowed the Opposition just three hours to analyse the report before the start of the debate, at which point, of course, the report would be put on public display. For those three hours two Opposition spokesmen from the Lords and two from the Commons (one Labour and one Liberal Democrat from each House) were allowed to study the report – in isolation, in different rooms, without telephones, tape recorders, assistants or notebooks.

The demolition of the unwritten constitutional right of the people of Britain to an opposing point of view was complete. Those rights cannot be recreated in the same format as before. It isn't possible to rebuild four centuries of independence invisibly created but visibly recognized by successive Governments in Britain solely by an act of will. For these things rest, in the final analysis, unless they are protected by law, upon a system of mutual respect, checks and balances operated by men and women who practise politics on a daily basis in the Chambers of both Houses. As Conservative Governments have increased their own power within the system, these checks and balances have been targeted and destroyed, without regard for either history or necessity. It took only a relatively brief period within the House of Commons to convince me of the absolute need now for our citizens to be protected from the state by the creation of a written constitution. The citizen is powerless against the modern state. If knowledge is power, the state's power is absolute, for the state now has access to every scrap of information about its citizens. And those citizens have no comeback, not even through the voices of their elected representatives. The Scott Report and its stage-managed publication showed that.

Government manipulation of information is hard to contest. In the pursuit of eternal power, the same political games are played with the larger audience, the country-wide electorate, as are played with Conservative Party supporters. False enemies are set up against whom the Government can score false victories. Inadequate or deliberately misleading statistics are published on matters of interest or importance to some part of the electorate. Take the question of nurses. Just before I entered Parliament in the 1987 election, there was a nationwide scare about insufficient numbers of nurses as a result of Government under-funding of the health service. The health minister announced, however, that there were 39,000 more nurses on duty now than there had been when the Conservatives took power in 1979. I used that figure in many speeches until a friendly Conservative MP who was retiring told me in deep despair that the statistics were politically corrupt. There were indeed 39,000 more nurses; but there were no more nursing hours, because all that had happened was that the same number of hours had been reconfigured into different shifts. The same volume of nursing was being undertaken; as shift times were shorter, there were more names on the roster, but they were not necessarily new ones.

The months passed. Paddy Ashdown, Paul Tyler and Malcolm Bruce (and by implication, the Liberal Democrat Party) and Britain's farmers were the only people to emerge with credit from the BSE crisis. After thirteen weeks the Government handed the BSE crisis management role to the NFU. It seemed to the farmers that this pinned the blame for the scheme's continuing and now inevitable failure on the NFU in advance. The farmers' tolerance was strained sometimes to suicide, particularly by the endless alterations to the rules in the Government's plans for the destruction of good cattle. They wondered, too, why the Government had failed to undertake any proper logistical organization: cattle from the south-west were being transported all the way to Cheshire for slaughter. Two and a half billion pounds was the midsummer madness figure for the cost of the disaster. The only people who gained were the abattoir owners, with the prospect of long queues of customers and a guaranteed good price, paid for by the Government, for a long while to come.

The summer wore on. Richard Holme was organizing our Oxford weekend to plan for the general election; I was a part of the team. Paddy Ashdown launched new proposals for constitutional reform, drawn up with Michael Ryle, former Clerk of the House and a close friend of my father. My office work calmed down. My staff had taken a sharp increase in their workload with professional competence and personal tolerance. Subsequently, Alicia retired, while Barbara went over to the AMAR office to take up a larger challenge. I accepted Liberal Democrat offers of help and took on Miranda, Eduardo and Dan. Cowley Street, the Liberal Democrat Head Office, was buoyant with young energy and idealism. The sterility of 32 Smith Square was in the past.

*

Inside the Chamber of the House of Commons, the digital clock flicked up 10 p.m. Outside, muffled from our hearing by centuries-old thick stone walls, Big Ben struck the hour. The Deputy Speaker called the vote. It was the end of a Liberal Democrat supply day, when my new party held the ring, choosing the subject on which to call the Government to account. Sitting on the green benches in the House with Menzies Campbell and David Steel, we talked about Gulf issues as we waited. Archie Kirkwood was counting the vote through. Diana Maddock, Ray Michie and Liz Lynne walked up the steps to vote. As I entered the 'Aye' Lobby with this friendly female group, Paul Tyler passed through. No wonder the south-west Conservatives were frightened by him. His prodigious grasp of subjects and tenacity in pursuit of them made him formidable. We were well served in the West Country by Liberal Democrats. Nick Harvey on my other northern flank was a superb performer. Matthew Taylor made up the quartet. Britain was shaded with gold from Newbury (my old home) to Land's End, the tip of Cornwall, through Liberal Democrat victories either on local councils or in Westminster. Not a bad score for a party only eight years old. There was all to play for, and I had made sure that my own efforts could be, once again, *pro bono publico*.

The small Liberal Democrat Whips' Office off the Members' Lobby was packed with colleagues doing their late-night chores. A weary trio of farming constituents emerged in Central Lobby. I took them to the Pugin Room to round off their Westminster visit. The monitor showed that the adjournment debate had started. There was one Opposition frontbench watcher, the Government Whip on duty and the minister concerned. Political night was setting in. The footfalls lessened, the debate wound to its end and the House rose. My old constituent and friend Mr Andrews woke up in his customary corner in Central Lobby, where he'd spent every parliamentary sitting day since 1961 writing a book, took up his bags and left. It was time to go home. I realized, of course, that in all the ways that mattered to my political life, I was at home already.

Epilogue

I have described the reactions of some parts of the parliamentary Conservative Party to my decision to resign their whip and join the Liberal Democrats. Here are some reactions of members of the public, many of them former Conservative supporters.

The passages reproduced below represent a small fraction of the postbag which arrived following the announcement of my decision. Many people objected particularly to the way in which the Conservatives chose to attack me. Many simply wanted to let me know that they agreed with my reasoning.

Of those who wrote to me, 23 per cent were against my move – most expressing this in abusive terms – but 77 per cent were in favour, of whom under one-quarter were already Liberal Democrats. A few of the thoughts of those who supported my decision follow.

*

As a former Chairman of Oxford Tory Reform Group, I made the same journey that you have now made. Like you, I had no doubt that, with the spirit of One Nation Conservatism all but extinguished in the modern Conservative Party, those values are now best expressed in Liberal Democracy.

Ian Huffer, Ludlow Constituency Liberal Democrat PPC

Just a quick note to say how much I admire your courage and conviction. I wish more people in politics were like you.

Television producer

When John Major announced soon after his election that we were to be at the heart of Europe and gave the clear impression that the confrontational politics of the Thatcher years were not to his liking, I joined the Conservative Party. He has been true to neither of these promises; I have not renewed my subscription this year.

Anon.

'I've little doubt that you will go far, you may even get to the top, but you will arrive without principles, integrity or honour and without ideas, and you will be surrounded by people of a similar ilk.'

Mr Bell of Ascot, said to John Major in his banking career 'If you want to get to the top you have to identify who has the power and join them, whether you agree with them or not.'

John Major talking to Mr Bell, reported in the same letter

I stood for Parliament as a Conservative in the 1970 general election . . . I saw how important it is for Great Britain to be a loyal, active and constructive partner in the European Union. I had remained a member of the Carlton Club throughout this whole period and from time to time stayed there, dining at the 'club table', which gives one the opportunity to talk and listen to opinions. In the last few years I became more and more dismayed by the anti-European, nay chauvinistic attitude of the newer members. Furthermore, they display a lack of concern for the poor and the sick which I found deeply offensive. One evening I told them that they were standing the Magnificat on its head and that it was the rich who are being filled with good things and the poor who are sent empty away. They claim Churchill as one of their heroes, but I told them that he would be ashamed of them.

William Morton, Lincoln

I just wanted to thank you for myself and the many thousands of ex-Conservative voters for your principled stand. I have watched and listened with dismay at the lurch to the right which has resulted in a lack of compassion and the destruction of our society.

Michael Dalley, Brighton

Under Major the downward rush has been even faster while the degree of sleaze (thanks to the press) has become more and more public.

James Stevens, North London

I used to vote Conservative, so did most of my family; my mother even used the front room of our house as a committee room for local Conservatives on election days, but that was many moons ago, when the Conservatives were caring and took the middle ground in most aspects of running the country. Now all we see from that party is greed, xenophobia and all the worst excesses of a party absolutely NOT LISTENING to what most caring people want from their leaders.

Denise Taylor, Berkshire

I've been a 'wettish' Tory all my life, but currently find myself in despair over the way much of the party seems to have lost its knowledge of how ordinary people think, work and vote. To me, too, Portillo's speech at the Party Conference was a final straw and a final nail in the coffin of something I once loved.

Scottish Tory

I must tell you that I too am now switching . . . I have seen the writing on the wall for some time which, I am sad to say, is full of ever-expanding cracks. Since the present incumbent in No. 10 took over he has allowed the Tory Party to crumble and degenerate into an elite group that caters solely for the upper classes and cares not a jot for the rest of society.

Kenneth Solly, West Sussex

We have been in the same boat and had to resign from the party. Nor do we regret it. There is no way we could support the Portillo persuasion and would spoil our own votes rather than risk any chance of the extremists gaining power.

Audrey Hull, Cambridge

As an old 'one nation' Tory I too have decided to leave the party. The party conference nauseated me. It is sad to think that Portillo's father and Howard's father were both refugees and found asylum here from extreme right-wing governments.

John Davies, Dumfriesshire

Although I have been an ideological Tory voter, I found Thatcherism to deteriorate into selfish materialism. 'Caring' is a tacky little word for a wholly admirable British tradition, apparently now extinct. 'Uncaring', however, is what we have now: a worse word and an indictment which should be answered.

Christina Gordon, West Sussex

Almost two years ago I resigned from the Conservative party after twenty-six years' involvement . . . The point of my exasperation came with John Major's shilly shallying on Europe because I believe in making a significant contribution in Europe, and I am sure from continental business contacts that our leadership would have been welcome in the aftermath of German reunification, but now most of our partners are as exasperated with this government as I am.

Don McCubbin, Merseyside

The Conservative Party . . . has become the party which does not listen to the people, and even when it does, rides rough shod over their views . . . I phoned Smith Square during the Tory conference to denounce their perceived and real heartlessness, in almost all spheres of British life – mental health, prisons, the

NHS, education, the arts, all reduced and demoralised – and said I could not vote Tory again.

Helen Mitchell, North London

When it comes to breaking commitments to the electorate, John Major is in a class of his own! . . . I also feel the disgust that you feel over the lack of commitment on Major's part to clean up the sleaziest aspects of Government. It came as no surprise to me to find that Major, having promised the opposite, was adept at sweeping the Nolan recommendations under the carpet. I expect that Major's political fear of upsetting those in the Conservative Party determined to protect their own established self-interest made this outcome inevitable.

Peter M. Jackson, Cheshire

I have been dismayed over many months now at the injustice of some Government policies. The Government seems to think that we are all selfish individuals who are only interested in our own incomes. I would gladly pay my taxes if I thought they were being spent fairly and that everybody contributed according to their levels of wealth.

Dr Stephen Saxby, Southampton

I know that it takes a lot of courage to undergo some drastic change of direction: perhaps even more so when one is convinced that the ship of state may be travelling in the wrong direction and carrying a lot of unwanted cargo – some of it pretty tainted and no longer too wholesome.

Martyn Lloyd, Suffolk

I come from a Tory-voting family who believe in freedom of choice and rewards for enterprise – but also in social justice.

Carol Williams, Northamptonshire

Both myself and my father have stopped voting Conservative for the very same reason. We feel they are too 'hard right'. Ironically, when John Major became PM we were relieved as we felt he would steer the party back to its central path away from the Tory right that was so prominent under Mrs Thatcher.

Sarah Bird, Essex

If Members of Parliament of all political parties were to follow your example and obey their conscience as opposed to the whip, then our democracy would be a healthier one.

Stephen McBride, London

I feel that blindly following one's party against one's conscience can lead one into the most appalling trouble (look at Germany in the 1930s, an extreme example but true enough).

Dr Rachel Dawson, East Anglia

It is very hard in a whipped party system to stand out against the tide.

Martin Bulmer, Thames Ditton

Emma Nicholson: A Political Chronology

Autumn 1975	Applies to join Conservative Central Office list of potential Parliamentary Candidates and is accepted
Spring 1976	Selected as Conservative Party Prospective Parliamentary Candidate for Blyth
May 1979	Adopted as Conservative Party Parliamentary Candidate for Blyth; fights general election unsuccessfully. Conservatives win election; Margaret Thatcher becomes Britain's first woman Prime Minister
June 1983	Conservatives win general election
July 1983	Appointed Conservative Party Vice-Chairman with special responsibility for women
March 1985	Selected as Conservative Party Prospective Parliamentary Candidate for Devon West and Torridge
May 1987	Marries Michael Caine. Adopted as Conservative Party Parliamentary Candidate for Devon West and Torridge
June 1987	Elected MP for Devon West and Torridge. Conservatives win general election
1987	Sits on various standing committees and statutory instrument committees
1987 onwards	Joins various backbench and all-party committees. Accepts a small proportion of honorary positions in charities and founds new ones. Joins the Lollards Group (a party club)

July 1987	Asked to resign as Conservative Party Vice-Chairman and does so
1988–92	Vice-President of the Conservative Technology Forum
1989	Introduces Computer Hacking Bill
1989–90	Industry and Parliamentary Fellowship with IBM
1989–90	Member of Standing Committee on European Community Documents
1990	Founding Chairman of All-Party Parliamentary European Information Market Group (EURIM)
1990–2	Member of Select Committee on Employment
July 1990	Introduces Access to Personnel Records (Employment) Bill
Sept. 1990	Visits Romania and subsequently founds All-Party Parliamentary Group on Romanian Children; launches associated appeal (raises £150,000)
Nov. 1990	Conservative Party leadership election. Supports Michael Heseltine. Mrs Thatcher resigns; John Major wins on second ballot
1991	Founding Chairman of ADAPT; organization raises £3 million
1991	Co-founder Cities in Schools (national truancy programme)
1991–5	Member of European Standing Committee A
1991–2	Chairman of Conservative Backbench Environment Committee (Secretary, 1990–1)
Jan.–Feb. 1991	The Gulf War
Aug. 1991	Visits Iran to assist Iraqi refugee situation; subsequently enters Iraq on a number of occasions
Sept. 1991	Founds AMAR Appeal to assist the Marsh Arabs of Iraq and refugees and displaced

	persons world-wide; Appeal has raised £4 million to date
Feb. 1992	Brings Amar to UK for surgery; with Michael, becomes responsible for his welfare
April 1992	Conservatives win general election
1992–5	Member of Medical Research Council
1992–6	Parliamentary Private Secretary to Michael Jack in the Home Office, Ministry of Agriculture, Fisheries and Food, and the Treasury
1992 onwards	Founds and chairs the All-Party Parliamentary British Iraq Group and the All-Party Parliamentary British Kuwait Group. Chairs the All-Party Parliamentary British Oman Group. Becomes Vice-Chairman, All-Party British Iran Group and Secretary or Treasurer to equivalent groups for Syria, Saudi Arabia and Yemen
1994	Secretary, then Treasurer, of the All-Party Parliamentary Parenting Group and member of other similar groups
1994–6	Treasurer of Positive European Group (Conservative backbench group)
1995	Joins Macleod Group (new Conservative backbench group)
July 1995	John Major resigns as Conservative Party leader then defeats John Redwood in subsequent leadership contest and reassumes position
Sept. 1995	Resigns as a Parliamentary Private Secretary
Oct. 1995–July 1996	Visiting Parliamentary Fellow, St Antony's College, Oxford
Late Dec. 1995	Has talks with Liberal Democrat Lord Holme and party leader Paddy Ashdown
29 Dec. 1995	Resigns Conservative Party whip, joins Liberal

	Democrat Party and takes their whip
Feb. 1996	Appointed Liberal Democrat Commons spokesman on overseas development and human rights
April 1996	Sets up AMAR Medical Aid project in Lebanon for displaced villagers after the Israeli 'Grapes of Wrath' military action

At present (mid-1996) holds approximately fifty charitable responsibilities

Index

Out of the blue...

INDIGO

the best in modern writing

FICTION

Nick Hornby *High Fidelity*	£5.99	0 575 40018 8
Kurt Vonnegut *The Sirens of Titan*	£5.99	0 575 40023 4
Joan Aiken *Mansfield Revisited*	£5.99	0 575 40024 2
Daniel Keyes *Flowers for Algernon*	£5.99	0 575 40020 x
Joe R. Lansdale *Mucho Mojo*	£5.99	0 575 40001 3
Stephen Amidon *The Primitive*	£5.99	0 575 40017 x
Julian Rathbone *Intimacy*	£5.99	0 575 40019 6
Janet Burroway *Cutting Stone*	£6.99	0 575 40021 8

NON-FICTION

Gary Paulsen *Winterdance*	£5.99	0 575 40008 0
Robert K. Massie *Nicholas and Alexandra*	£7.99	0 575 40006 4
Hank Wangford *Lost Cowboys*	£6.99	0 575 40003 x
Biruté M. F. Galdikas *Reflections of Eden*	£7.99	0 575 40002 1
Stuart Nicholson *Billie Holiday*	£7.99	0 575 40016 1
Giles Whittell *Extreme Continental*	£6.99	0 575 40007 2

*IN*DIGO books are available from all good bookshops or from:

Cassell C.S.
Book Service By Post
PO Box 29, Douglas I-O-M
IM99 1BQ
telephone: 01624 675137, fax: 01624 670923

While every effort is made to keep prices steady, it is sometimes necessary to increase prices at short notice. Cassell plc reserves the right to show on covers and charge new retail prices which may differ from those advertised in the text or elsewhere.